Walter William Skeat

An English-Anglo-Saxon Vocabulary

Walter William Skeat

An English-Anglo-Saxon Vocabulary

ISBN/EAN: 9783337075484

Printed in Europe, USA, Canada, Australia, Japan

Cover: Foto ©Paul-Georg Meister /pixelio.de

More available books at **www.hansebooks.com**

AN

ENGLISH–ANGLO-SAXON

VOCABULARY.

COMPILED BY

THE REV. WALTER W. SKEAT, M.A.,

ELRINGTON AND BOSWORTH PROFESSOR OF ANGLO-SAXON.

Cambridge:

AT THE UNIVERSITY PRESS.

1879

Cambridge:
PRINTED BY C. J. CLAY, M.A.
AT THE UNIVERSITY PRESS.

INTRODUCTION.

On the appearance of Mr Sweet's Anglo-Saxon Reader in 1876, it occurred to me that an English index (if I may so call it) to the words contained in the admirable Glossary appended to it would be useful, at any rate to myself. In the course of 1878 I made such an index. On looking it over, I at once observed that some very common and characteristic words were wanting in it, on account of the necessarily limited nature of the selections. It then occurred to me that many of these could be readily supplied by help of the index to Mr Sweet's History of English Sounds. I accordingly went through that index, and so filled up some of the gaps. In a *very* few cases I passed over the words thus indicated, because the word was unimportant or the form a little doubtful.

Hence the present list contains *only* such English words as occur (1) in the explanations of Anglo-Saxon words in Sweet's Glossary to the Reader (first edition); and (2) nearly all the words given in his History of English Sounds. The result is a vocabulary which gives some account of most of the more important words of the language; and shews, on the one hand, what words are still in use nearly unchanged, and on the other, what ideas are expressed by totally different terms in the modern and in the oldest English.

Limited as is the vocabulary, it has at any rate this advantage, viz. that all the Anglo-Saxon words cited are *real* ones, for which actual authority can be adduced. The passages in which they occur can be found by the references in the Glossary to the Reader;

1—2

or else, when the word is but slightly changed, by reference to the dictionaries of Bosworth, Lye and Manning, or Ettmüller. As it is chiefly in the former case that the *construction* of the word may require illustration, it is easy to turn to the passages cited and observe any peculiarity of usage. It will at once be seen that, from the way in which the list has been compiled, it is necessarily scanty and imperfect. It is merely a handy list, intended for my own use and for that of a few friends and students.

CAMBRIDGE,
April 14th, 1879.

N.B. When modern English verbs and substantives are not distinguished as such, the *verbs* may be readily known by the fact that the Anglo-Saxon infinitive mood ends in *-an.* It may also be noted that additional Anglo-Saxon words may often be found under synonymous English ones. Thus *to bid* is *beódan;* and, by looking under *command,* we also find *hátan.*

VOCABULARY.

A

a, án
abandon, forlǽtan
abbess, abbudisse
abbot, abbod
abject, heán
able, to be, cunnan
abode, wunung
about, ymbe, ymb, embe, w. acc.;
    onbútan, ymbútan
above, ofer, ufan, búfan ; (of superiority) tóforan ; adv., uppe;—
    from above, ufan
abroad, út, útanbordes, úte
abstain from, wiðbredan, refl.
abundance, genyht
abuse, v., hirwan
accessible, gefére
accomplish, æfnan, bewitian, geforðian, þurhteón ; fullgán, w. dat.
according to, be
account, gerád
account, v., tellan
accurately, gewyrdelice
accursed, unlǽd
accusation, wróht
accuse, gewrégan, forwrégan ;—accuse of, gestǽlan, w. dat.
ache, æce, ece
acknowledge, oncnáwan
acorn, æcern, æcirn
acquire, gewinnan, strínan
acre, æcer
act, v., dón
action, weorc
adder, nædre
addition, eáca
adhesive, clibbor

AID

admonish, gemanian
adorn, besettan, gefrætwian, gehlæstan, gerénian, girwan, glengan, teón (weak verb), weorðian, wurðian
adorned, gehroden, geatolic
adulterer, hóring, ǽbreca
adultery, hór, forligere, ǽbryce
advance, wadan
advent, tócyme
adversary, andsaca, wiðersaca
advice, lár, lárcwide, rǽd
advise, gerǽdan, rǽdan, lǽran
adze, adesa, adese
afflict, eglan, gebrócian, gecwilman, gedreccan, geswencan, gewǽgan, genearwian, geþryscan, þryccan
afflicted, gedréfed
affliction, bróc, hearm, weorc
aforesaid, se foresǽda ; foresprecen
afraid, forht, ofdrǽdd
afraid, to be, forhtian, ondrǽdan
after, æfter ; (of time), ofer ; (of place) on lást, w. dat.;—after that, ðæs ðe
afterwards, eft, siððan, ðæs, æfter ðám
again, eft, eft ongeán
against, on, ongeán, ongén, wið, w. acc.; (hostilely), tógeánes
age (old age), ildu ; (growing old), ealdung
agitated (in mind), ástyred
agree to, geþwǽrian, geþwǽrlǽcan
agreeable, gecwéme
agreement, treów, wedd, gecwidrǽden
aid, fultum

5

ail, eglan
air, lyft
akin, gesibb
alas, wá lá wá
alder, alr
alderman, ealdorman·
ale, ealu
alight (from a horse), líhtan
alike, gelíce
alive, cwic,'cucu
*all,*eall;—*most of all,* ealra mǽst;—
  at all, áwiht, tó áhte
allow, áliffan, *w. dat. of pers. and*
  acc. of thing; lísan, lǽtan, geþáf-
  ian, geþwǽrian
allure, spanan
almighty, eallmihtig, eallwealdend
almost, forneáh;—*almost all,* swíð-
  ost ealle
alms, ælmesse
almsgiving, ælmesgifu
alone, án
along, be
alongside of, tóemnes, *w. dat.*
also, ealswá, eác, éc; eác swilce,
  eác swá; swilce, swilce eác
altar, weofod
alter, áwendan
although, ðeáh, ðéh, ðeáh ðe
always, ealne weg, ealneg; ǽfre;
  symble; gehwǽr
am, eom
ambition, rícetere
ambush, sǽtung
amid, onmiddan
amidst, tómiddes
among, ongemang, mid, betweó-
  num
an, án
ancestors, ildran
and, and, ond
angel, engel
angels, race of, engelcynn
angelic, engellic
anger, torn, grama, irre
angle; see hook
angrily, torne, irringa
angry, irre, gram, wráð, ábolgen,
  gebolgen
angry, to be, ábelgan
animal, neát   •
ankle, ancleow
announce, bodian, *w. dat.;* ábeód-
  an
annul, ásdlian, áwǽgan; (*annul
  laws*), forniman
anon, on án

answer, v., andswarian, andwyrdan
answer, s., andswaru, andwyrde
ant, æmette
anvil, anfilte
any, ǽnig
any one, hwá
anything, wiht, wuht
anywhere, áhwǽr, hwǽr
apart, sundor
ape, apa
apostate, aposíata
apostle, apostol
appear, æteówian; þyncan, *impers.,
  w. dat.*
apple, æppel
apply, áteón;—*apply oneself to,*
  befeolan, *w. dat.*
appoint, settan, dihtan, sceáwian;
  gelagian, genamian, gescirian,
  gcteohhian
approach, neálǽcung, upgang
approach, v., geneálǽcan
archangel, heáhengel
archbishop, arcebiscop
ardour, inbryrdnis, onbryrdnis
are, sind, sindon, beóð (*Northum-
  brian* aron)
arise, árísan; (*be born*), wacan
ark, earc
arm, earm
arm, v., girwan, gewǽpenian
armour, reáf, herereáf; firdham,
  firdhrægl, eorlgewǽde
army, here, herefolc, folc, fird,
  sweót
around, ymbe, ymb, embe; ymbút-
  an, onbútan
arouse, weccan
arrange, fadian, áredian
array (oneself), trymian, trymman,
  refl.
arrow, flán, strǽl; hildenædre;
  also arewe
art, cræft, searu
art (2 p. s. pres. of verb), eart
artifice, searu, sirwung
as, swá; (*according as*), ðæs ðe;
  swilce, *w. indic.; as...as,* swá...
  swá;—*as if,* swilce, *w. subj.;*—
  as soon as, sóna swá. [*as* = eal
  swá]
ascend, stígan
ascension, upástigennis
ascent, upstige
ascribe, getitelian
ash, æsc
ashamed, to be, scamian, *impers. w.*

acc. of person and gen. of thing ;
forscamian
ashes, æscan, axan, ascan (*pl.*)
ask, áxian, ácsian, áscian ; biddan,
w. acc. of pers. and gen. of thing ;
fricgan, frignan
asking, áxung, ácsung
aspen (tree), æsp, æps
ass, assa
assail, on sittan
assemble, gegadrian, gesamnian.
assembly, gesamnung, gemót
assistance, fultum
associate, s., gegada, eaxlgestealla
associate with, tó geþeódan
association, geþeódnis
astrologer, tungolwítega
at, æt, tó ;—*at all,* wiht, wuht,
     wihte ; *and see all*
atone for, ongildan
attempt, onginnan
attendant, foregenga, geóngra
aught, áwiht, áht
aunt, módrige
authority, onweald
autumn, hærfest
avail, dugan
avarice, gítsung
avaricious, feóhgífre
avenge, áwrecan, wrecan
avenger, wrecend
avoid, forbúgan, forcirran, forfleón
await, bídan, *w. gen.,* ábídan, on-
     bídan
awake (arouse), weccan, áweccan :
     (*to be awake*), wacian ; (*to become
     awake*), onwacan, onwacnan
away, onweg, aweg, forð, fram,
     ðanon
awe, ege, egesa
awl, awel
axe, eax
axle; see shoulder
aye; see ever

B

back, bæc, hrycg
back again, eft
backwards, ofer bæc, under bæc
bad, yfel, earglic, fracod
bad, to become, yfelian
badly, yfele, yfle
bag, fætels
bailiff, geréfa, túngeréfa ; wícgeféra
bake, bacan
bale, bealu

baleful, bealufull, bealu
balk (ridge of land), balca
ban (proclamation), gebann
band, bend
bane, bana
banish, áflíman
bank (of river), eá-stæð
banner, cumbol, þúf
banquet, symbel
baptism, fulluht
baptize, fullian
bar, grindel
bare, bær.
bark, v., beorcan
barley, bere
barm (yeast), beorma
barn, bern
barrenness, unwæstm
barrow (hill), beorh
bast, bæst
bath, bæð
bathe, baðian ; *trans.* gebeðian
bathing, beðung
battle, gefeoht, hild, orett, here,
     gewinn, getoht, tohte ; beadu,
     beadulác ; æscplega, ecgplega,
     gúðplega, wígplega
battle-field, wæl, wælstow, mæðel-
     stede
be, wesan, weorðan, beón
beacon, beácen
beam, beám
bean, beán
bear, s., bera
bear, v., beran ;—(*a child*), geberan
beard, beard
bearer of a corpse, lícmann
beast, deór, neát, níten ; (*wild
     beast*), wilddeór
beat, beátan, cnyssan, þerscan
beautiful, fæger, hiwbeorht, freólic,
     scíne, torht, wlitig
beauty, fægernis, wlite, beorhtnis
because, for ðám ðe, for ðý ðe, ðæs
     ðe, ðý
beckon, bécnan, beácnian
become, weorðan
bed, bedd, rest
beer, beór
beetle (insect), bétel, bítel
beetle (rammer), býtel
befit, gerísan
before, adv., fore, foran, beforan, ǽr
before, prep., for *w. dat.,* beforan;
     (*of time*), ætforan, *w. dat.,* tófor-
     an, *w. dat.,* onforan, *w. acc.*
beforehand, ætforan

beg,bedecian(*Greg. Pastoral*,p. 285)
beget, strínan
begin, onginnan, beginnan
beginning, fruma, frymð, onginn,
  ord   .
behave, gebǽran, féran
behest, hǽs
behind, adv., behindan, æt hindan,
  on swaðe ;—*from behind*, æftan
behind, prep., beæftan
behold, behealdan, sceáwian
behold! efne! lá! hwæt!
behove, gebyrian, behófian
being (creature), wuht, wiht
belch, bealcettan
belief, geleáfa
believe, gelífan
believing, geleáffull, gelífed
bell, bella (*or* belle)
bellow, bellan
belly, wamb, belg
belong, gebyrian, belimpan
beloved, leóf
belt, belt
bench, benc
bend, bendan ; (*bow down*), lútan
beneath, adv., neoðan ; *prep.* beneoð-
  an, *w. dat.*
benefit, v., fremian, *w. dat.*
benefit, s., fremsumnis, fremu, þearf
benevolent, welwillende .
bequeath, becweðan
bereave, bereáfian
berry, berige
beset, bestandan   .
besides, adv., git, tóeácan ; *prep.*
  (*w. dat.*), eác, tóeácan
besiege, ymbsittan, besittan
besom, besma
best, betst, sélest
betray, forrǽdan, beswícan ; (*a city*),
  becirran
betrayal, swicdóm
better, adj., betera, sélra ; *adv.*, bet
between, betweónum, betwux, be-
  twix
betwixt, betwux, betwix
bewail, cwíðan
beyond, begeondan
bid, bebeódan, beódan
bide, bídan
bier, bǽr
bill (weapon), bill
bin, binn
bind, bindan, cnyttan, sǽlan ; (*as
  prisoner*), wélan
birch, beorc

bird, fugol
birth, ácennednis, gebyrd ; (*time
  of*), gebyrdtíd ;—*of noble birth*,
  æðelboren
birthplace, cennungstow
bishop, biscop
bishopric, biscopstól
bit, v., (*to furnish a horse with a
  bit*), bǽtan
bitch, bicce
bite, bítan
bitter, biter
black, blæc, sweart
bladder, blædr
blade (of grass), blæd
blain, blegen
blame, v., tǽlan
blast, blǽst
bleach, blácian
bleak (*pale*), blǽc, blác
bleat, blǽtan
bleed, blédan ; swǽtan (*poet.*)
blend, blandan
bless, geblétsian
blessed, gesǽlig, eádig
blessing, blétsung
blind, blind
blind, v., áblendan
blindly, blindlice
bliss, bliss
blithe, blíðe
blood, blód ; *also* heolfor, swát (*poet.*)
bloodshed, blódgyte
bloody, blódig ; *also* dreórig, heol-
  frig, swátig (*poet.*)
bloom, v., geblówan
bloom, s., blóma
blossom, blóstma
blow, v., bláwan ;—*blow upon*, be-
  wáwan
blow (as a flower), blówan
blow, s. (*stroke*), drepe, sweng
boar, bár, swín ; (*wild*), eofor
board, bord
boar-spear, eoforspreót
boast, gebeótian
boasting, beót, gilp
boat, bát
bode, bodian
bodily, líchamlic
body, líc, líchama, flǽschama, bodig
boil, weallan
bold, beald, gebilde, céne, dyrstig,
  fram, hwæt, snell, strang ; arod, cáf
boldly, bealdlice, cénlice, framlice,
  cáflice
boldness, dyrstignis, hwætscipe

bolster, bolster
bolt, bolt (?)
bond, bend, clamm
bone, bán
book, bóc
boon, bén [boon = Icel. bón]
boot (remedy), bót
booty, lác, húð
bore, borian
borough, burh
borrow, borgian
bosom, bósm, bearm
both, begen ;—both...and, ǽgðer...
   ge, ge...ge
bottom, botm ; (of a lake, &c.),
   grund
bottomless, grundleás
bough, telga, bóh
boundary, mearc
bow, v., gebúgan, búgan ;—bow
   down, trans., onhildan; intrans.,
   hnígan, onlútan
bow (for shooting), boga, flánboga
bower, búr
bowl, bolla
boy, cnapa, cniht
braid, bregdan
brain, brægen
bramble, bremel (or brémel)
branch (of a tree), telga
brand, brand
brandish (a sword), bewindan
brass, ǽr, bræs
brave, gód, heard, hwæt, strang,
   stíðmód, hrór ; róf (poet.) ; un-
   earg ; and see bold
bravehearted, heardmód, stíðmod
bravely, heardlíce, þegenlíce ·
bravery, hwætscipe ; and see bold-
   ness
breach, bryce ; (of agreement),
   weddbryce ; (of law), lahbryce
bread, breád
breadth, brǽdu
break, brecan ; (become broken),
   sprengan ;—break to pieces, tó-
   brecan, forbreótan ;—break asun-
   der, intrans., tóberstan
breast, breóst
breastplate, byrne, byrnham
breath, blǽd, fnǽst, brǽð
breathe, orðian
breeches, bréc (pl. of bróc)
breed, brédan
brew, gebreówan
bride, brýd
bridegroom, brýdguma

bridge, brycg
bridle, brídels (or brídels)
bright, beorht, scír, torht, hádor,
   leóht, leóhtlic
brightly, beorhte, hádre
brightness, beorhtnis
bring, bringan, ætberan, lǽdan ;—
   bring about, gewendan ;—bring
   forth (child), cennan, ácennan,
   oncennan, tíman, tydran ;—bring
   up, fédan
broad, brád
brood, bród (unauthorized)
brook, v.; see use
brook, s., bróc
broom (plant), bróm
broth, broð
brother, bróðor
brow, brú
brown, brún
buck, bucca
build, timbrian, timbran, átimbran,
   bytlan, arǽran ; settan ; (firmly),
   trymman
building, getimbre, getimbrung, ge-
   bytle
bullock, bulluca
bundle, byndel
burden, byrðen
burn, intr., beornan ; trans., bær-
   nan, ǽlan, forswǽlan ;—burn up,
   forbærnan (trans.), forbeornan
   (intrans.)
burning, s, bryne
burst, berstan ;—burst forth, bre-
   can ;—burst out, áberstan
bury, byrgan, bebyrgan, bedelfan
busy, bysig
but, ac
butter, butera (a borrowed word
   from Latin)
buy, bycgan, gebycgan ;—buy off,
   forgildan
by, be, bi ; (by means of), þurh ;
   fram, w. pass. verb

C

cable, scipráp
calamity, gelimp
calf, cealf
call, ceallian ; (to exclaim), clipian,
   cleopian ; (to name), gecígan ;
   (to call out), hríman
callow (bald), calu
calumny, hól ; (attack on character),
   onscyte

9

camp, wíc, wícstow, firdwíc
campaign, s., fird
campaign, v., firdian
can (I), cann
candle, candel (*Latin*)
canon, canon (*Lat. and Gk.*)
capacity, mægen
captivity, hæftníd
capture, v., niman, fón
care, caru, cearu, heord
care, v., hogian ; (*to reck*), meornan, récan ; (*to care about*), carian, onmunan ; (*to take care of*), gíman, *w. gen.*
careful, carfull, smeálic
careless, réceleás, gímeleás, orsorh, wanhýdig
carelessly, unwærlice
carelessness, unwærscipe, gímeleást
carnal, flǽslic
carrion, ǽs
carry, beran, ferian, lǽdan, wegan ; *carry off or away*, álǽdan, offérian, áwegan
cart, cræt
carve, ceorfan
castle, castel (*Latin*)
cat, catt
catch, gelǽcan
cathedral, mynster
cattle, ceáp, feoh, feó, neát, · níten, orf, hryðer
cattle-plague, orfcwealm
cause, dón, *w. infin.*
cause, s., intinga
cauterize, fortendan
cave, scræf
cease, áblinnan, gestillan
cease from, geswícan, *w. gen.*
celebrate, mærsian
celebrated, mǽre
certain one, án, sum
certain of, gewiss, *w. gen.*
certainly, gewisslice, georne
chafer (insect), ceafor
chaff, ceaf
chain, clamm, bend, racente
chain, v., gehæftan
chalk, cealc
chamber, búr, cófa, reced
chamberlain, búrþegn
champion, cempa
change, v., áwendan, behwirfan ; (*change to the worse*), onwendan
change, s., edwenden ; (*vicissitude*), gebregd ; (*reverse*), edhwirft
chapman, ceápmann

character (nature), hád
charge, have in, bewitan
chariot, cræt
charitable, cystig, ælmesgeorn
charity, ælmesgifu
cheap ; see purchase, sb.
cheek, ceáce
cheer, fréfran, gefréfrian, árétan
cheese, cése
chew, ceówan
chicken, cycen
chide, cídan
chilblain ; see blain
child, bearn, cild, eafera
childhood, cildhád
chill, freórig
chill, s., céle
chin, cinn
choice, dóm
choice thing, cyst
choke, forþrysmian
choose, ceósan, geceósan
chough, ceó
church, cirice, circe ; (*congregation*), gelaðung
cinder, sinder
circuit, ymbgang, ymbhwirft, begang
circumference, ymbgang
citizens, burhleóde, burhsittende, burhwaras
city, ceaster, burh
clamour, hreám, gebǽre
claw, clawu (*or* cláwu)
clay, clæg
clean, clǽne
clean, adv., clǽne
cleanness, clǽnnis
cleanse, clǽnsian
clear (evident), sweótol, swutol ; (*used of the voice*), beorht
clearly, sweótollice
cleave (adhere), clifian
cleave (sever), cleófan
cleave asunder, tócleófan
clerical, gehádod
clew, cliwe
cliff, clif
climb, climban
climb up, stígan
cling, clingan
clip (to embrace), clyppan
close, v., lúcan, belúcan ; (*close up a road*), forwyrcan
cloth, cláð
clothe, scrýdan
clothes, gewǽde

cloud, wolcen. [*The A. S.* clúd = *mass of rock*].
clout, clút
clover, clæfre
cluster, clyster
coal, col
coat, tunece, cyrtel, pád
cock, hana, coc
cockchafer; see chafer
cock-crow, hancréd
cockle; see corn-cockle
cold, ceald
cold, s., céle
collect, gegadrian, gesamnian
colour, hiw
coloured, fáh, fág
colt, colt
comb, camb
combat (*single*), ánwíg
come, cuman, becuman; (*to the throne*), fón tó ríce
comely, cymlíc
comfort, frófor
comfort, v.; see cheer
coming, cyme, tócyme
command, v., beódan, hátan, bebeódan
command, gebod, bebod, diht, hǽs, geweald
commit, betǽcan
common, gemǽne; — *in common*, gemǽnelice
companion, gesíð, geféra, geneát
company, geférscipe
compel, geneádian, genídan, fornídan
complain, mǽnan, besprecan
complete, v., fullfremman, fullwyrcan, þurhteón
compose (*write*), gedihtan
comrade, wilgehléða
conceal, bedirnan, bediglian, míðan
conceive (*be pregnant*), geeácnian
concerning, of
condemn, fordéman
condition (*state*), hád
conduct, faru, fær, drohtnung
confess, andettan
confine, beclýsan
confirm, áfæstnian, gefæstnian
congregation, laðung, gelaðung
conquer, álecgan, gehnægan, gewildan, ofweorpan; (*land*), gegán
conscious, gecnáwe, *w. gen.*
consecrate, gehálgian
consent to, geþáfian

consenter (*consenting person*), geþáfa
consider, beþencan, þencan, hogian, smeágan, smeán, ásmeágan, geondsceáwian, geondþencan
consolation, frófor
console, fréfran, gefréfrian
constancy, ánrǽdnis
contain, befón
contemplation, smeágung
contempt, forsewennis, forhohnis, oferhygd
contend, sacan
continual, singal
continually, singallice
continue, wunian, þurhwunian
continuously, ánstreces, on án
contrary to, ofer
contrive, áþencan
control, wealdan
conversion, gecirrednis
convert, gehwirfan, behwirfan, gebígan
cook, s., cóc (*Latin*)
cool, cól
cool (*grow cool*), cólian
corn, corn
corn-cockle, coccel
corner, hyrne
corporeal, líchamlic
corpse, hrǽw, hrá, líc
correct, gerihtan
cote (*cot*), cóte
could, cúðe
council, rǽd, rún
councillor, wita, rúnwita, rǽdbora
counsel, rǽd
count, ríman
countenance, andwlita
country, land, eard, molde
courage, mód, þrymm; ellen (*poet.*)
course, ryne
court, hof; (*inclosure*), edor
cover, belecgan, þeccan, beþeccan, helan, wríhan, bewríhan, bewyrcan;—(*cover over*), oferhelman; (*cover with rime*), behreósan
cow, cú
cowardice, irgðu
cowardly, earg, earglic
cowslip, cúsloppe
crab (*fish*), crabba
crackle (*as flames*), brastlian
cradle, cradol, cildcradol
craft; see skill
cram (*stuff*), crammian
crane, cran

11

crave, crafian
create, gesettan, gescippan, onstellan, trymman
creation, gesceap, gesceaft, gescapennis, frumsceaft
Creator, metod, meotod, scippend
creature, wiht, wuht, gesceaft
creep, creópan, snícan
cress, cerse, cærse
crib, cribb
crime, synn, undǽd, morðor, gylt, fácen, firen, leahtor, mán, mándǽd
criminal, s., wearg, sceaða
cringe (bow, fall), cringan, gecringan
cripple, crépel
crooked, wóh
crop (of wheat), wyrt
crop (of a bird), cropp
cross, ród, gealga
cross, sign of the, ródetácn
cross oneself, sénian
crow, cráwan
crowd, gemang, hwearf
cruel, wælhreów, réðe, gram, grimm, wráð, unswǽslic
cruelly, þearle
crumb, cruma
crush, tócwýsan
crutch, cricc
cry (clamour), cirm
cry aloud, hríman, cirman
cultivate, gebúan
cunningly, geáplice
cup, bune, cuppe
curse, s., curs
curse, v., cursian
cursed, áwirged
curtain, fleóhnett
custody, heord
custom, þeáw, sidu, gewuna ; *(evil custom),* unsidu
cut, ceorfan, heáwan, bítan, sníðan, sceran
cut away, áceorfan onweg
cut off, beceorfan, *w. acc. of pers. and instr. of thing*
cut through, forceorfan

D

daily, dæghwámlice
daisy, dæges ége
dale, dæl
dam up (a river), forwyrcan

danger, frécednis ; *(sudden danger),* fǽr
dangerous, frécne
dare, durran, néðan ; *I dare,* ic dearr
dark, deorc, mirce, sweart, wann, heolstor, þeóstre, þeósterfull
darkness, heolstor, þeóstru
darling, deórling
dart, daroð
daughter, dóhtor
dawn, uhte, ǽrdæg, dægréd
dawn, v., dagian
day, dæg ; dógor *(poet.)*
day's work, dægweorc
dead, deád, forðgewiten, unlifigende
deadly, deáðbǽre, cwealmbǽr
deaf, deáf
deal, dǽl
dear, deóre, dýre, leóf
death, deáð, gewitennis, forðfór, forðsíð, hinsíð, swilt, hryre, fill, cwealm, cwild
death, doomed to, fǽge
death-day, deáðdæg
decay, forrotian, fúlian, brosnian
decay, s., brosnung
deceit, swicdóm
deceitful, swicol
deceive, beswícan, bepǽcan
decide, gescádan, geceósan, rǽdan, gerǽdan
decline, óðfeallan, wanian
decree, gerǽdan, rǽdan, gescirian, déman
decree of fate, gesceaft
deed, dǽd, þing
deem; see doom
deep, deóp, steáp
deeply, deópe
deer, deór
defeat, v., forsleán
defeat, slege
defeated, sigeleás
defend, werian, bewerian, gebeorgan, ealgian
defender, weriend
defile, besylian, besmítan, wemman ; gefýlan
defilement, wamm, gewemmednis
degenerate, ábroðen
delay, ildan, latian, uforian
delay, ildung
delve, delfan
demand, girnan, *w. gen.*
demon, sceocca, scucca
den, denn

deny, áleógan, *w. dat. of pers. and
acc. of thing;* forsacan
depart, gewítan
departing thence, ðanonweard
departure, útgang
depending on, gelang æt
deplore, bewépan
deprive of, beniman, benǽman, *w.
gen. or instr.;* bedǽlan, belíðan,
w. gen.; besnýðian, *w. instr.;*
áfirran, *w. dat. of pers. and acc.
of thing;* bescirian, *w. gen. of
thing;* óðwendan, *w. dat. of pers.
and acc. of thing*
depth, dípe, dýpe
derision, hócor, hosp
derisive, hócorwyrde
descendant, maga
desert (waste), wésten
desert, adj., wilde
desert (merit), gewyrht
deserve, earnian
design, geþeaht, rǽd
desire, girnan, *w. gen.;* gítsian ;
willan ; wilnian, *w. gen. or acc.;*
gelystan, *impers. w. acc. of per-
son and gen. of thing*
desire, willa, lust, wilnung
desirous, georn, *w. gen.*
despair, ormódnis
despairing, ormód
despairing of, orwéne, *w. gen.*
despise, forhogian, forseón
despiser, oferhoga
destroy, fordón, spillan, forspillan,
forwyrcan, forniman, forfaran,
ámirran, ábreótan, ádilgian, tó-
weorpan
destruction, forwyrd, cwild
determine, gemearcian
detest, onscunian
detestable, onscunigendlic
devastate, hergian
devastation, hergað, hergung, for-
hergung
devil, deófol
devil, possessed by a, deófolseóc
devilish, deófolcund, deófollic
devise, ácræftan
devour, forswelgan, fretan
dew, deáw
die, steorfan, sweltan, cwelan, á-
cwelan, geendian, gefaran, gewít-
an, forðfaran
difficult, earfoðe, earfoðlic
difficulty, with, uneáðe, uníðelice
diffidence, unbildo

dig, delfan
digging, gedelf
dignity, geþyngðo, geþyncð, weorð-
fullnis
diligently, gecneordlice
dill, dile
dim, dimm
diminish, trans. and intrans., ge-
wanian
din, to make a, dynian
dint (a blow), dynt
dip, dífan ; dyppan
dire, atol, slíðen
direct, gerihtlǽcan, gewissian, wís-
ian, tǽcan
direction, gewissung
disciple, leornere, leornungcniht,
geóngra
discipline, þeódscipe
discourse, cwide
discover, áfindan, onfindan
discredit, unhlísa
disease, cóð, ádl, uncóðu
diseased, ádlig
diseased, to be, ádlian
disengage oneself from, geæmtigian;
reflex. w. gen.
disgrace, scamu, scand
disgraceful, scandlic
dish, disc
dishearten, geirgan
dislike, unþanc
disperse, intr., tófaran, tóféran ;
trans., tósendan
display, gesweótolian, geswutolian,
eówan
display, s., wæfersín
displease, mislícian, *w. dat.*
dissimulate, lytigian, lícettan
distant, firlen
distension, tóbláwennis
distinct, sweótol, swutol
distinguished, geþungen
distribute, dǽlan
district, sceát, scir
district, governor of a, scirmann
disturbance, unstillnis
ditch, díc
dive, dúfan
divide, dǽlan, tóniman, tódǽlan
divine, godcund, dryhtenlic
divinely, godcundlice
divinity, godcundnis
division, dǽl
do, dón, gedón
dock (plant), docce
doctrine, lár

doe, dá
dog, hund
doing amiss, miswende
dole, gedál, dǽl
dominion, onweald, ríce
doom, dóm
doom, v., déman
door, duru
doubt, tweó, tweónung
doubt, v., tweógan, tweón, *w. gen.;*
  tweónian, *impers.*
doubt, without, untwílice, untweó-
  gendlice
doubtfully, tweólice
dough, dáh (?)
doughty, dyhtig
dove, culfra; dúfe (*or* dúfa)
down (hill), dún
downwards, of dúne, neoðan, niðer
drag, dragan, teón
dragon, draca, wyrm
draw, dragan, teón
draw (sword), gebregdan, ábreg-
  dan, teón
draw near, getengan
dread, v., onþrácian, ondrǽdan
dreadful, onþrǽce
dream, v., gemǽtan
dream, swefn
dreary, dreórig
dress, wǽd, gewǽde, wǽfels, hrægl,
  reáf, scrúd
drink, drincan, súpan ; (*drink up*),
  gedrincan ; (*give to drink*), drenc-
  an
drink, s., drenc
drinking, gedrinc
drive, drífan, drǽfan ; (*away*), áfýs-
  an, fordrífan, ádrífan
drop, dropa
dropsy, wæterseócnis
drove, dráf
drown, trans., ádrencan
drunk, druncen
dry, dryge
dry up, ádruwian
due, gerisen
dull, dol
dumb, dumb
dun (brown), dunn
during, under, *w. dat.*
durst (I), dorste
dust, dust
duty, riht
dwarf, dweorg
dwell, wunian, wícian, eardian, ge-
  búan, búgian

dwell in, trans., healdan
dwelling, hám, wíc ; inn, geard,
  hof, eard, geset, gesteald, wunung
dwelling-place, eardgeard
dyke, díc

E

each, ǽghwilc, *w. gen.;* ǽlc, ge-
  hwilc, ǽghwæðer, ǽgðer, gehwæð-
  er
each one, gehwá
eager, georn, geornfull, geornfullic,
  fús
eagerly, geornfullice, geornlice,
  georne
eagle, earn
ear, eáre
earl, eorl
early morning, ærnemergen
earn, geearnian
earnest, eornest;—*in earnest,* on
  eornest, eornestlice
earnestly, eorneste
earth, eorðe, grund, folde, molde,
  hruse, middangeard
earthdweller, foldágend, foldbúend,
  eorðbúend
earthly, eorðlic
easily, eáðe, sófte
east, eást
east, from the, eástan
east, to the, wið eástan
Easter, Eástron (*pl.*)
Easter-day, Eásterdæg
eastward, eásteweard
easy, eáðe, éðe
eat, etan
eaves, efes
ebb, s., ebba
ebb away, áebbian
ecclesiastical, circlic
edge, ecg
eel, ǽl
egg, æg
eight, eahta
eighty, hundeahtatig
either (of two), áhwæðer, áwðer
either...or, oððe...oððe, óðer...óðer
eke, v., écan
elder, ildra
elders, ildran
elder-tree, ellen
eldest, ildesta
eleven, endlufon
eleventh, endlyfta
elf, ælf

ell, eln
elm, elm
eloquence, getyngnis
else, elles
elsewhere, ellor
embrace, clippan, ymbclippan
embrace, s., fæðm
emmet, æmette
emperor, cásere
employment, notu
empty, æmtig, ídel
encamp, gewícian, sittan
enclosure, haga
encourage, trymian, trymman, ge-
  bildan
end, ende, geendung
end, v., endian
end, bring to an, onwendan
endless, ungeendod
endure, bídan, *w. acc.;* þolian
enemy, feónd, feóndsceaða, sceaða,
  mánscaða
English, Englisc
English, the, Engle, Angle
English language, Engliscgereord
enjoy, brúcan, *w. gen.;* neótan,
  w. gen.
enjoyment, notu
enlighten, onlíhtan
enmity, feóung, ofþanca
ennoble, gedírsian, gedýrsian
enough, genóg
enrage, gremian
enslave, geþeówian
ensnare, besirwan
enterprise, onginn
entice, spanan, gewéman
entirely, mid ealle, ealles, eallunga,
  æghwæs
entrails, innoð
entrance, inngang, instæpe
entrust, befæstan, *w.dat.;* bebeódan
equinox, emniht
ere, ær
erect, áræran
err, misféran
err, to cause to, dwelian
errand, ærende
error, gedwild
erst, ærest
escape, ætberstan, óðwindan, losian,
  berstan; —*escape from*, ætwindan,
  w. gen.
establish, settan
eternal, éce
eternally, écelice
eternity, écnis

eucharist, húsl
evangelical, godspellic
evangelist, godspellere
even, efen, emn
evening, æfen
eventide, æfentíd
ever, æfre, á, áwa; —*for ever*, tó
  ealdre
every one, æghwá
everywhere, æghwær, gehwær, ofer
  eall
evident, sweótol, swutol, open
evident, to make, geswutolian
evil, yfel
evil, s., yfel, bealu
evil-doer, mánfremmende
ewe, eówe
examine, ásmeágan
example, bigspell, bysen, bysnung
example, to give an, bysnian
excel, oferstígan
excellence, duguð
excellent, æðele, ænlic, unforcúð, in-
  dryhten, geþungen
except, búton
excessive, ungemetgod, swíðlic
excessively, ungemet, ungemetlice,
  swíðlice, oferlice, ungefóge
exchange (barter), s., gewrixle
excite, onstyrian
exculpate oneself, betellan, *reflex.*
excuse, geládian, forlætan
exhalation, steám
exhausted, ágoten, *w. gen.*
exhausted, to become, áteorian
exhort, gemanian
exile, wræcsíð
expedition, síð, rád; (*military*),
  fird
expel, ádræfan
expend, áspendan
explain, gereccan
exploration, sceáwung
explore, cunnian
expound, áreccan
extend, brædan, gerýman, ástreccan
extensive, wídgille
external, úteweard, útanweard
externally, útane
extinguish, ácwencan, ádwæscan
extreme, ýtemest
eye, eáge

F

face, andwlita
fade away, wanian

fail, swícan, geswícan, *w. dat. of person;* álicgan
fain, fægen
fair, fæger, scíne
fairness, fægernis
faith, treów, treówð, getreówð, getrýwð, geleáfa
faith, want of, geleáfleást
faithful, getreówe, hold
faithfully, getreówlice
fall, feallan, dreósan, gedreósan, hreósan, áhreósan; (*bow down*), cringan; (*fall away*), áfeallan
fall, s., dryre, hryre, fill
fallow, fealu
false, leás
falsehood, leásung
fame, hlísa
familiar, cúð
family, mægð, cynn, híred
family, member of a, híwa
famine, hungor
famous, namcúð, mære, mǽrlic, bréme, gefrǽge
famous, to make, mǽran, gefrǽgnian
far, feorr;—*from afar,* feorran
fare, v., weorðan, *impers. with acc.;* (*to go*), faran
farthing, feorðling
fast (*fasting*), fæsten
fast, adj., fæst
fasten, fæstnian
fastness, fæsten
fat, fæt
fate, wyrd, síð; (*decree of fate*), gesceaft
father, fæder·
fathom, fæðm, fæðmrím
fault, gylt
favour, ést, liss, hyldo
fawn (*as a dog*), onfægnian
fear (*be afraid*), onscunian, *reflex.;* ofdrǽdan, ondrǽdan
fear, óga, ege, egesa; (*fright*), fyrhto, forhtung; (*sudden danger*), fǽr
fearful, egesfull, egeslic
fearfully, egeslice
fearless, unforht, unforhtmód
feast, gebeórscipe, wist
feast, v., wistfullian
feather, feðer
fee (*property*), feoh
feed, fédan, áfédan
feel, félan
fell, áfillan

fell (*skin*), fell
fen, fenn
fern, fearn
fervour, wilm
festival, freólstíd
festivity, plega
fetch, feccan, fetian
fetter, fetor, racente
feud, fǽhð
fever, fefor, fefor-ádl
fever, to have a, hriðian
few, feá
fickle, ficol
fiddler, fiðelere
fidelity, treówð, trýwð, getreówð, getrýwð
field, feld, æcer, wang;* (*field of battle*), wæl
fiend, feónd
fierce, gram, grimm, irre, réðe, hreóh, hreó, stíð, stíðmód
fiercely, wráðum, irringa, stíðlice
fierceness, réðnis
fifteen, fiftíne
fifth, fifta
fifty, fiftig
fight, feohtan, winnan, sacan
fight, s., gefeoht, feohte, camp, campwíg, tohte
fighter, cempa
file (*rasp*), feól
fill, fyllan, áfyllan
fill, s., fyllo
film, filmen
fin, finn
find, findan, métan, begitan; (*find out*), onfindan, áfindan
finger, finger
finish, v., geendian, betýnan, þurhteón
fir, furh
fire, fýr
fire-gleam, fýrleóht
firm, fæst, trum
firmly, fæstlice, fæste
firmness, fæstnis
first, forma, fyrmest, fyrst
first, adv., ǽrest
fish, fisc
fisher, fiscere
fishing, fiscoð
fist, fýst
fitly, sidelice
fitting, gelimplic
five, fíf
flame, blǽst, líg
flat (*applied to land*), filde

flatter, óleccan
flattery, óleccung
flax, fleax
flea, fleá
flee, fleógan, gefleóhan
fleece, flýs
fleet, adj., fleótig
flesh, flǽsc
fleshly, flǽsclic
flight, flyht, fleám
flight, to put to, áflígan, áflíman, geflíman, fýsan
flint, flint
flitch, flicce
float, fleótan
flock, flocc
flood, flód
flooded, fléde
floor, flór, flett, heallwudu
flourish, þeón, geþcón, wridian, geblówan
flourishing, geblówen
flow, flówan; (*as a river*), feallan, irnan
flow of the tide, flód; (*stream*), gang
fluctuate, wealcan
fly, s., fleóge
fly, v., fleógan
foal, fola
foam, fám
fodder, fódor
foe, feónd
fold, fealdan
folk, folc
follow, folgian, fyligan
following, æftera
folly, unsnotornis, unwísdom, unræd, hygeleast, dysig
food, fóda, mete, metsung, æt, nest, feorm, bigleofa
food, want of, metelóst
foolish, dysig, dysiglic, dwǽs, dol
foolishly, dollice
foot, fót
foot-measure, fótmǽl
footprint, spor
for, for, tó
forbid, forbeódan
force, níd
force, by, níde
ford, ford
forefather, forðfæder
foreign, fremde, welisc, elþeódig
foreigner, wealh
forest, wudu, holt, weald, wuduholt
forge, ásmiðian

forged, geþuren
forget, forgitan
forgive, forgifan
forgiveness (of sins), forgifennis
former, ǽrra
formerly, geára, geó, giú, iú, gefyrn, ǽr ðissum
forth; see forwards
forthwith, sóna, ædre, ðǽrrihte ánunga, semninga
fortification, geweorc
forty, feówertig
forwards, forð
foster-father, fóstorfæder
foul, fúl
found (a town), ásettan, settan; (*a building*), trymman
foundation, gesetnis, staðol, weallsteall
fountain, willa
four, feówer
fourfooted, fiðerféte
fourteen, feówertíne
fourth, feórða
fowl; see bird
fowler, fuglere
fox, fox
foxglove, foxes glófa
fragment, bryce
fragrance, stenc
frailty, tydernis, hnescnis
frankincense, récels
free, freó
free from, leás
freeze, freósan
fresh, fersc
Friday, frigedæg
friend, freónd, wine
friendless, freóndleás
friendly, freóndlic, hold
friendship, freóndscipe
fright, fyrhto, forhtung
frightened, áfirht
frivolity, ídelnis
frog, frocga
from, fram, of, æt; (*to learn from* = geliornan æt)
frost, forst
frosty, hrímig
frozen, froren
fruit, wæstm, ofet, bléd, blóstma
fry, gehirstan
frying, hirstung
fryingpan, hearstepanne
full, full
fully, fullice
funeral, lícþenung

funeral pile, ád, bǽl
furlong, furhlang
furnace, ofen
furrow, furh
further, furðor
further away, ufor
furze, fyrs
future, tóweard
future, *s.*, forðgesceaft

G

gain, gewinnan, strínan
gall, gealla
gallows, gealga, galga
game, gamen
gang, gangan
gannet, ganet, ganot
gape, geapian
garment, scrúd
gate, geat
gatekeeper, geatweard
gather (*flowers*), gadrian ; (*collect*),
    gegadrian
gaze, starian
gear, gearwe
gem, gimm, gimmstán
general, *s.*, folctoga
general (*common*), gemǽne
generally, gemǽnelice
gentle, rów, líðe, geswǽs, smylte
gently, líðelice
gesture, gebǽre
get, gitan
get at (*reach*), gerǽcan
ghost, gást
giant, eoten, ent, þyrs, gigant
gift, gifu, lác, leán
gigantic, eotenisc
gild, gyldan
girdle, gyrdel
girl, mægden, mǽden, mægð
give, gifan, sellan ; (*permit to have*),
    onlíhan, *w. dat. of pers. and gen.
    of thing;* (*grant*), unnan, *w. dat.
    of person and gen. of thing*
give away, forgifan, forgildan
give up, ofgifan, oflǽtan
giver, brytta (*poet.*)
glad, glæd, glædmód, fægen, blíðe,
    rót
gladden, gegladian, árétan
gladly, glædlice, rótlice
glass, glæs
gleam, scíma, glǽm
glede (*hot coal*), gléd
glee, gliw

glide, glídan
glitter, lixan
gloaming, glómung
gloom, glóm
gloomy, *to become*, gesweorcan
glorify, mǽran, mǽrsian
glorious, þrymmfæst, þrymmfull,
    þrymmlic, þryðlic, mǽre, mǽrlic,
    blǽdfæst, tírfæst, torhtlic
gloriously, hlísfullice, dómlice
glory, wuldor, tír, hréð, dóm, lof,
    mǽrðu, blǽd, þryðu, þrymm,
    weorðmynt, wurðmynt
glory, *eager for*, dómgeorn
glove, glóf
gluttony, oferfyll
gnash the teeth, gristbítian
gnashing of teeth, gristbítung
gnat, gnæt
gnaw, gnagan
go, gán, gengan, cuman, faran, féran,
    ferian, steppan, wadan, scríðan,
    teón, wendan (*reflex. or intrans.*)
go in a track, spyrian
go without, forþolian, *w. instrum.*
go wrong with, mislimpan, *impers.
    w. dat.*
goad, gád
goat, gát
God, god
god-child, godbearn
goddess, gyden
godfather, cumpæder
God-fearing, godfyrht
godson, godsunu
gold, gold
golden, gylden
goldsmith, goldsmið
good, gód, gódlic, til, ǽrfæst
goodly, gódlic
goodness, gódnis
goods, gód
goose, gós
gore (*blood*), heolfor
gorse, gorst
gory, heolfrig
gospel, godspell
gout, gihða
govern, gewealdan
government, steór
grace, ést ; (*of God*), gifu
gracious, hold
grandfather, eald fæder
grant, unnan, getíðian, *both w. gen.
    of thing and dat. of person;* (*grant
    as a favour*), tíðe fremian
granted, gifeðe

grasp, gegrípan, grápian, fón, hafenian
grasp, fæðm, gráp, clamm
grass, græs
grave, græf
gravel, sandceosel, greót
gray, græg
gray (of hair), hár
gray-haired, blandenfeax
great, greát, micel
greater, mára
greatest, mæst
greatly, miclum
greatness, micelnis
greedily, grædiglice
greediness, gífernis
greedy, grædig, gífre
green, gréne
greet, grétan
grief, weá, sár, hearm
grief, tidings of, weáspell
grieve, sárettan
grievous, swár, sár, láð, wráðlic
grievously, weorce
grim, grimm, grimmlic
grind, gegrindan
grip, gripe, gráp
gripe, gegrípan, grípan
groan, gránian
groaning, gránung
groom, guma
grope, grápian
ground, grund, flór, folde
groundsel, grundeswelge
grove, bearu
grow, weaxan, grówan ; (*grow up*), áweaxan ; (*grow over*), beweaxan
growth, wæstm
grudge, of þanca, inca
guard, v., behealdan, healdan, warian
guardian, weard
guardianship, weard
guest, gist, flettsittende
guidance, gewissung
guide, gewissian, wísian
guild, gild
guilt, gylt, scyld
guilty, scyldig, forscyldigod
gut, gutt

H

habit, gewuna, þeáw
had, hæfde
hail, hagol
hailstorm, hagolfaru

hair, hǽr ; *head of*, feax
half, healf
hall, heall, sele, sæl, seld
hallow, gehálgian
halt (lame), healt
hammer, hamor
hand, hand ; folm (*poet.*)
hand over, tó handa lǽtan, árǽcan
handgrasp, mundgripe
handiwork, handgeweorc
handle, helf
handy (near), gehende
hang, trans., áhón, gehón ; *intrans.* hangian
happen, gelimpan, getímian, weorðan, wesan
happiness, sǽl, gesǽlð
happy, gesǽlig, eádig
harbour, port
hard, heard
harden, áhirdan
hardhearted, heardheort
hardheartedness, heardheortnis
hardly, uneáðe
hardness, heardnis
hardship, earfoð, geswinc
hare, hara
harlot, miltestre
harm, hearm, bealu
harp, hearpe
harp, v., hearpian
harper, hearpere
harping, hearpung
harrow, s., herewe, herwe (?)
harrow, v., ettan
harry, hergian
harrying, hergung, hergað
hart, heorot
harvest, ríp, ríptíma, hærfest
haste, ófost ;—*with haste*, ófstlice
hasten, éfstan, onettan, fundian ; fýsan (*reflex.*)
hastily, recene, ricene
hat, hæt, hætt
hate, hatung, hete
hate, v., hatian, láðian, feón
hateful, láð, láðlic
hater, hata
hatred, anda, níð
haughty, oferwlenced, ofermód
have, habban
haven, hæfen
hawk, hafoc
hay, híg, hég
hazel, hæsel
he, hé, se
head, heáfod, hafola

headland, næss
headless, heáfodleás
head-man (leader), heáfodmann
heal, hǽlan
health, gesundfullnis, hǽlo
healthy, hál, onsund, gesund, gesundfull, hálwende
heap, heáp
hearing, gehírnis
hearken, hércnian, hýrcnian
heart, heorte, mód, hyge ; sefa, ferhð (*poet.*)
hearth, heorð
heat, hǽte, hǽtu
heat, v., onhǽtan
heath, hǽð
heathen, hǽðen
heathendom, hǽðenscipe
heave, hebban
heaven, heofon, heofone
heaven, kingdom of, heofonríce
heavenly, heofonlic
heavy, hefig, swár
hedge, haga
heed, gíman, *w. gen.;* hédan, *w. gen.*
heel, hóh, héla
height, héhðu, heáhnis, heánnis
hell, hell, hellewíte
hell-fire, hellbryne
hell-gate, helldor
helmet, helm
help, help, fultum, frófor, ár, duguð, rǽd
help, v., helpan, *w. dat. or gen.;* fylstan, *w. dat.;* gelǽstan, *w. dat.;* forstandan, *w. dat.;* gefultumian
helve, helf
hemp, hanep, hænep
hen, henne
hence, heonan
henceforth, heonan forð
her, acc. case, hí ; *dat.,* hire
herdsman, swán, hirde
here, hér
heretic, gedwolmann
heritage, láf, irfe, irfeweardnis
hesitate, wandian, ildan
hew, heáwan ; (*hew down*), áheáwan
hidden, dirne, dígol
hide, v., gehýdan, behýdan, helan
hide (skin), hýd, fell
hie, higian
high, heáh, heálic
hill, beorg, dún, hlǽw, hlinc, munt, hyll
hill-side, hlið

hilt, hilt (*often in pl.*)
him, dat., him ; *acc.,* hine
hinder, gelettan, *w. acc. of pers. and gen. of thing;* hremman ; (*hinder from or in*), ámirran, *w. gen. of thing*
hip (dog-rose), heópe, hiópe
hip (thigh), hype
hire, hýrian, áhýrian
his (own), sín
historian, þeódwita, wyrdwritere
historical, gewyrdelic
history, stær
hither, hider
hoard, hord
hoard, v. hordian
hoarfrost, hrím
hoarse, hás
hoary, hár
hold, healdan
hold out (endure), þolian
hole, hol
hollow, hwealf
holly, holegn
holy, hálig
home, hám, eard, cýð, cýððu ;— *at home,* æt hám
home-coming, hámcyme
homewards, hámweard, hámweardes
honest, getreówe
honestly, getreówlice
honey, hunig
honour, ár, árweorðnis, mǽð, weorðmynt, wurðmynt, weorðscipe, wurðscipe
honour, v., árian, weorðian, wurðian, árweorðian, mǽðigian
honour, worthy of, árweorð
honourable, árweorðfull, weorðfull, wurðfull
honourably, weorðlice, wurðlice, árweorðlice
hood, hód
hoof, hóf
hook, hóc
hook (fish-hook), angel
hop, hoppian
hope, hopa, hyht
hope, v., hopian, gehyhtan
hopeless of, orwéne, *w. gen.*
horn, horn
horse, hors, mearg, mearh ; eoh (*poet.*), wicg (*poet.*)
host (vast number), unrím, ungerím
hostage, gísel
hostile, láð, fág, hetol, wráð, unhold

hostility, fǽhð, wiðersac, unfrið
hot, hát
hotly, háte
hound, hund
hour, tíd
house, hús, inn, botl
household, híred
householder, bónda, húsbónda
how, hú
however, hwæðre, ðeáhhwæðere, swáðeah
hue, hiw, bleoh
hue, bright of, hiwbeorht
human, mennisc
humble, eáðmód
humble, v., geeáðmédan
humbly, eáðmódlice
humiliate, gehínan, forbígan
hundred, hund, hundteóntig
hunger, hungor
hunt, huntian
hunter, hunta
hunting, huntað
husband, ceorl, wer
husbandry, tilung, teolung
hustings, hústing
hymn, lofsang

I

I, ic
ice, ís
icicle, célegicel, ísgicel
idle, ídel
idleness, ídelnis
idol, deófolgild, hearg
idolater, deófolgilda, hǽðengilda
idolatry, hǽðengild
if, gif
ignominious, heánlic, huxlic
ignominiously, bismerlice
ignorance, nytennis
ignorant, nyten
ill (sick), mettrum, untrum, seóc
ill, to make, geuntrumian
ill, adv., yfele, yfle
illness, untrumnis, mettrumnis
illuminate, onlíhtan
ill-use, gehínan, misbeódan, tucian
image, onlícnis
immediately, recene, ricene
immense, ormǽte
impel, fýsan
impending, onsǽge
improper, ungerisenlic
improve (become better), gódian ; *(make better),* bétan

imprudence, unwísdom
impure, unsífre, wammfull
in, in, *prep.;* on, *prep.;* inn, *adv.*
in exchange for, wið, *w. dat.*
in front of, tógeánes, *w. dat.*
in order that, tó ðæm ðæt
in, to get, feolgan
incense, récels
inch, ynce
incite, áweccan, stihtan, onbryrdan, onbærnan
incline, búgan, gebúgan ; *(intrans.),* onlútan
incline oneself (bow down), hildan, *reflex.*
incomparably, unwiðmetenlice
increase, weaxan ; *(trans.),* geícan
increase, s., eáca
incredible, ungelífedlic, ungelífendlic
incredibly, ungefrǽglice
indeed, witodlice, eornestlice, húru
indescribable, unásecgendlic
indignation, níð
infirm, untrum
infirmity, untrumnis, untrymnis
inflame, onǽlan, onbærnan, onhǽtan
inhabit, warian
injure, wirdan, wyrdan, sceððan, derian
injurious, deriendlic
injury, hearm, daru, láð, teóna, byrst
injustice, unriht
inn, inn
inner, innera
innermost, innemest
innocence, bilewitnis
innocent, bilewit, unscæððig, unscyldig, unforworht
innocently, bilewitlice
insignificance, wácnis
inside, innan
inspect, geháwian
inspiration, onbryrdnis
institute, gestǽlan, stǽlan, settan
instruct, tǽcan
instruction, láreówdóm
insult, v., bismerian, bismrian, scendan
insult, s., hosp, hócor, bismer, teóna
intelligence, andgit, gewitt
intelligent, andgitfull
intend, gemyntan, þencan, hogian
intense, ormǽte
intercede for, þingian, *w. dat.*

intercept, offaran
internal, inweard
interpret, gereccan
interpreter, wealhstód
into, intó, in, on, inn on
intolerable, unáberendlic
invite, gelaðian .
involuntarily, ungewealdes
inward, inweard
inwardly, inweardlice
iron, íren
iron, adj., íren, ísern
is, is
island, ígland, icgað, igeoð
it, hit
ivy, ifig

J

jaw, ceafl
jeweller, gimmwyrhta
join, gefégan
journey, síð, síðfæt, fær, faru
journey, v., síðian
joy, bliss, blíðnis, wynn, hyht, mirgð,
    dreám, gliw, willa
joyfully, wynnum, hyhtlice
joyless, wynnleás
judge, déma, dćmend
judge, v., gedéman
judgment, dóm
just, riht
justice, gerihte

K

keel; see ship
keen (bold), céne
keep, healdan, behealdan; cépan
kernel, cyrnel
kettle, cetel, cytel
key, cǽg
kill, cwellan, ácwellan, ácwilman,
    ádídan, áfillan, bewegan, forweg-
    an, forspillan, heáwan, geheáw-
    an
kin, cynn
kind, hold
kind (nature), gecynd
kindly, árlice
kindness, mannþwǽrnis
kindred, cynren
king, cyning, drihten, dryhten, weald-
    end; freá (*poet.*)
kingdom, cynedóm, cyneríce, ríce
kinsman, mǽg
kinswoman, máge
kiss, cyssan

kiss, s., coss
kitchen, cycene
kith, cýð
knave; see boy
knead, cnedan
knee, cneów
knife, seax
knight; see boy
knit, cnyttan
knock, cnucian
knock against, hnítan
knoll, cnoll
knot, cnotta
know, cnáwan, gecnáwan, cunnan,
    gecunnan, witan; — *I know,* ic
    wát; —*I know not,* ic nát
know, not to, nytan
know assuredly, tócnáwan
knowledge, cræft
known, cúð, gecnáwen
known, to make, cýðan

L

labour, geswinc
lack, onsín
ladder, hlæder
lade, hladan
lady, hlǽfdige
lair, leger
lake, lagu, mere
lamb, lamb
lame, lama
lament, heófian, gnornian, rárian
lamentation, heófung, gnornung ·
lamp, leóhtfæt
land, land ; (*native*), éðel
language, sprǽc, gereord, geþeóde
lank, hlanc
lap, bearm
larboard, bæcbord
lark, láwerce
last, ýtemest, latost
last (to endure), lǽstan
late, adv., late, síð
Latin, lǽden
laugh, hlihhan
laughter, hleahtor
law, gerihte, gesetnis, lagu ; (*of
    God*), ǽ
lawfully, lahlice
lay, lecgan
lay down, álecgan
lay low (make to sink), gesǽgan
lay waste, áwéstan, íðan
layman, lay, lǽwed
lead, lǽdan

lead (*metal*), leád
leader, heretoga, folctoga, healdend, heáfodmann, ræswa (*poet.*)
leaf, leáf
leaky, hlece
lean, adj., hlǽne
lean, v., hlǽnan
leap, hleápan
leap up, áhleápan
learn, leornian ;—*learn by enquiry*, gefrignan, geáxian
learned, gelǽred, wís
learner, leornere
learning, leornung, lár
least, læst
leather, leðer
leave, lǽfan ; (*behind*), lǽtan
leave, s., leáf
lee (*shelter*), hleów
leech (*physician*), lǽce
leek, leác
legion, werod
lend, líhan, lǽnan
Lent (*spring*), lencten
less, læssa, adj.; læs, adv.
-less (*suffix*), -leás
lessen, trans. and intrans., gelytlian
lest, ðý læs ðe
let, lǽtan, forlǽtan ;—*let us*, uton, w. inf.
letter, ǽrendgewrit
letters (*writings*), stafas, pl.
lewd (*ignorant*), lǽwed
lick, liccian
lid, hlid
lie (*tell lies*), leógan
lie (*lie down*), licgan, gelicgan ; (*lie in wait for*), sǽtan
lief, leóf
life, líf, gást, blǽd, feorh, ealdor, sáwul
life-days, lífdagas (*pl.*)
lifeless, ealdorleás, sáwulleás, orsáwle
lift, hebban, áhebban
light, s., leóht
light (*of weight*), leóht
light (*of brightness*), leóht
lighten (*make lighter*), gelíhtan
like, gelíc, w. dat.; onlíc
likeness, onlícnis, gelícnis
likewise, swá same
limb, lim, lið, gesceap
lime (*for mortar*), lím
lime-tree, lind
linden-tree or wood, lind

lineage, strenge
linen, s., lín ; adj., línen
link (*ring*), hlence
lion, leó
lip, lippa
list (*edge of cloth*), list
listen, gehlystan
lithe, líðe
little, lytel
little, adv., lyt, lythwón
little one, lytling
live, libban
livelihood, bigleofa
liver, lifer
lo! lá!
load, v., hladan, gehlæstan
loaf, hláf
loam, lám
loan, lǽn
loathe, láðian, hatian
loathsome, láð
lobster, lopystre
lock, v., lúcan
lock of hair, locc
lodge, innian
lofty, steáp, uplic
long, lang
long, adv., langlice
long ago, gefirn
long-lasting, langsum
look, lócian, wlítan
loose (*loosen*), forlǽtan, álísan, onwindan, onlǽtan
loquacity, ofersprǽc
lord, hláford, . helm, onwealda ; hearra, freá (*poet.*); (*the Lord*), dryhten
lordly, dryhtlic
lore, lár
lose, leósan, forleósan, beleósan, w. instr.
loss, lyre
lost, to be, losian
lot, hlot
loud, hlúd
loudly, hlúde
louse, lús
lout (*to bow down*), lútan
love, lufe, lufu, myne, liss
love, v., lufian
lover, freónd
low (*as a cow*), hlówan
lukewarm, wlæc
lurk, lútian
lust, lust
-ly, -lic, -lice (*for* -líc, -líce)
lying (*act of*), leger

M

mad, wód
madness, wódnis
magistrate, ealdormann
maiden, mægden, mǽden
mail, coat of, hcrebyrne, herenett, heresirce, liðusirce
main (strength), mægen
majority, heáfodgcrím
make, macian, scippan, wyrcan
maker, wyrhta
male, wǽpnedmann
male-child, hysecild
malefactor, wearg
mallow, mealwe
malt, mealt
man, mann, manna, ceorl, guma, wer, secg, scealc, magu, esne; *also,* eorl, rinc, æðeling (*poet.*)
manhood (state of being a man), menniscnis
manifold, manigfeald
mankind, manncyn
manner, wíse
manners (morality), þeáwas, *pl.*
many, manig ; fela, *w. gen.*
mar (to spoil), merran
march, steppan
mare, mere
mark, mircels ; (*ornament*), mǽl
mark out, gemearcian
marriage, gifta (*pl.*); ǽ
marrow, mearh
marry, wífian; geǽwnian, *w. dat.*
marsh, mersc
marten, mearð
martyr, martyr
martyr, v., gemartyrian
martyrdom, martyrdóm
marvel, wundor
marvellous, wundorlic
mass (Lat. missa), mæsse ; *mass-priest,* mæssepreóst
massive, greát
mast (of ship), mæst, segelgird
mate (companion), gemaca
maternal, módorlic
matins, uhtsang
mature, to become, gerípian
maw, maga
may (to be able), mugan ; *pres.* ic mæg; *pret.* ic mihte; (*may be allowed*), mótan ; *pres.* ic mót, *pret.* ic móste
me, mé, mec
mead (drink), medu, meodu

meal (repast), gereordung, mǽl
meal (flour), melu
meal, to take a, snǽdan
mean (insignificant), wác, wáclic ;
   (*disgraceful*), heán
mean (to intend), mǽnan
meanwhile, betwux ðisum
measure, gemet
measure, v., metan
meat, mete
mediation, þingung
mediator, forespreca
medicine, lǽcedóm
meditate, þencan
meed (reward), méd
meet, gemétan
meeting, gemót
melody, swég, swinsung, hleóðor
melt, meltan
member, lim
memorable, þancwirðe
memory, myne, gemynd
men, men; *also* firas, niðas, ilde
   (*all poet.*) ; *see man*
mend, gebétan
merciful, milde, mildheort
mercy, mildheortnis, milts, miltsung, ár
mere (lake), mere, lago
merit, earnung, gewyrht
mermaid, merewíf
merry, merg, blíðe
message, gebodscipe, ǽrende
messenger, boda, ǽrendraca, ár, bydel
methinks, mé þyncð
mid, adj., midde
middle, middel
midge, mycg
midnight, middeniht
might, miht, meaht
mighty, mihtig, þearlmód
mild, milde, smylte
mile, míl, mílgemearc
milk, meolc
mill, mylen
mind, mód, geþanc, sefa, módsefa, gewittloca, gehyge, hyge, hréðer; ferhð (*poet.*)
mindful, gemyndig, gemun
mine, mín
mingle, mengan
ministration, þegnung, þénung
minster, mynster
mint (plant), minte
mint (for money), mynet
miracle, tácen

mirky, myrce, þeóstre
mirth, mirgð
mischief, anda, yfel, unrǽd
misdeed, misdæd
miser, gítsere
misery, wracu, wræc, irmðu
misfortune, ungelimp, ungesǽlð, láð
mishap, ungelimp
mist, mist, genip
mistletoe, misteltán
misty, grow, genípan
mixed, geblanden
moderate (small), mǽte, medmicel
moderate, v., gemetgian
moderation, gemetgung
moisture, wǽta, steám
mole (a spot), mál
moment, in a, bearhtme
monastery, mynster
monastic, mynsterlic, munuclic
monastic orders, munuchád
Monday, mónan-dæg
money, feoh, feó, sceatt
money-changer, mynetere
moneyless, feohleás
monger (chapman), mangere
monk, munuc, mynstermann
monster, aglǽca, elwiht
month, mónað
mood; see mind
moon, móna
moor, mór
morality, sidu
more, mára; *adv.*, má; — *much more*, micle swíðor
morning, morgen, morgentíd; *(early)* uhte
morsel, snǽd
mortal, deádlic
moss, meós
most, mǽst; — *most of all*, eallra swíðost
moth, moððe
mother, módor
motion, síð
mould (earth), molde
mound, hlæd, hlǽw
mountain, beorg, munt
mountain-stream, firgen-streám. [*Firgen* only occurs in compounds.]
mourn, meornan, gnornan
mourning, gnornung
mouse, mús
mouth, múð; *(of a river)*, múða
move, styrian, ástyrian, hréran; *(intrans.)*, wagian

movement, power of, féðe
mow, máwan
much, unlytel; micle, *w. comparatives*
multitude, menigu, heáp, worn; *(host)* duguð
munificence, gumcyst
murder, morð, morðor, morðdǽd, cwalu, slege, mannsliht
murderer, bana, cwellere, morðorwyrhta, mannslaga
murmur, murcnian; *(murmur at)*, bemurcian
must, I, ic sceal; *cf.* ic móste
mutter, clumian
my, mín
myrrh, myrre
mystery, rún

N

nail, nægel
nail, v., næglian
naked, nacod
name, nama
name, v., genamian, genemnan; *(call by name)*, hátan
nap (to slumber), hnæppian
narrate, reccan, áwrítan
narrative, racu, spell, gesetnis
narrow, nearu, enge, smæl
narrowly, nearulice
nation, þeód, þeódscipe, leódscipe, mægð, dryht, dryhtfolc
native, landbúende
native land, cýð, cýððu, éðel
nature, gecynd
naught, náwiht
nave (of a wheel), nafu
near, neáh, néh; gehende, *w. dat.*
nearly, wel
nearly every, gewelhwilc
neat (cattle), neát
necessary, nídbeþearf
necessity, níd, nídþearf
neck, heals, sweora; hnecca
need, níd, nídþearf, þearf
need, v., þurfan, *w. gen.*
need, I, ic þearf, *w. gen.*
needle, nǽdl
needy (in want), þearfende
neglect, forlǽtan, forgíman
neigh, hnǽgan
neighbourhood, neáwist, neáwest
neither, náhwæðer, nóhwæðer, náwðer; *neither...nor*, náwðer ne... ne

ness (headland), næss
nest, nest
net, nett
nether; see downwards
nettle, netele, netle
never, næfre
new, niwe
next, adv., æt néhstan
nigh, neáh
night, niht
night, by, nihtes
nightingale, nihtegale
nightly, nihtlic
nine, nigon
ninety, hundnigontig
ninth, nigoða
no, ná, nese;—*no one*, nán, nǽnig
nobility, æðelu
noble, s., æðeling
noble, æðele, þryðlic, torht, torhtmód, indryhten
nobly, weorðlice, wurðlice
noise, gebræc, breahtm
noise, to make a, hlýdan
none (no one), nán
noon, nón
north, norð, norðdǽl
north, from the, norðan
north of, be norðan, *w. dat.*
northern, norðern
northward, norðeweard, norðweard, norðweardes
nose, nosu
not, ná, ne;—*neither...nor*, ne...ne;
—*not at all*, náwiht, nealles, nálæs, mid nánum þingum; —
not only, ná ðæt án
nothing, náwiht
nourish, fédan
now, nú;—*now that*, nú
nowhere, náhwǽr
nun, nunne, mynecen
nut, hnutu

O

oak, ác
oats, áte
oar, ár
oath, áð
obedience, gehírsumnis
obey, gehírsumian, *w. dat.; folgian*, fyligan
obstinacy, þweorhnis
obtain, begitan, gerǽcan
occasion, cirr, sǽl, mǽl
occupied, pp., ábysgod

occupy (a country), gesittan, gerídan
ocean, brim, holm, geofon, gársecg
odour, stenc
of, of
off, of
offer, gebeódan; (*offer sacrifice*), offrian
offering, lác
office, ambiht
officer, geréfa
offspring, ofspring
often, oft, gelóme, gelómlice, geneahhe
oh! eálá
oil, éle
old, eald, unorne ; gamol (*poet.*)
old age, ildu
on, on, uppon, ofer
once, áne síðe ;—*at once*, recene, ricene
one, án ; (*indef. pron.*), man
one of six, sixa sum
only, ánga ;—*not only*, ná ðæt án
onslaught, gúðrǽs, beadurǽs
onwards, gegnum
open, v., openian, ontýnan, onlúcan ; (*forcibly*), tóslítan
open, open
openly, openlice
opinion, dóm
opportunity, rúm
opposite to, wið, *w. dat.*
opposition, wiðersæc
oppress, gehefgian, geþryscan
or, oððe
orator, þyle
order, endebyrdnis
ornament, hyrst, geréne, wrætt ; (*pl.*), frætwa
ornamental, wrættlic
other, óðer
otherwise, elles
otter, otor
otter, belonging to an, yteren
ought, v., áhte
our, úre
out, út, úte
out of, út of
outer, útera, úttera
outlaw, útlah
outlawed, fág
outside, út, útan, útane, úte
outside, adj., úteweard, útanweard
outside of, wiðútan, *w. dat.; búton*
oven, ofen
over, ofer

overcome, ofercuman, oferwinnan, oferswíðan
overlaid (with gold), begoten
overrun (a country), gefaran, ofergán
overthrow, ofweorpan
overturn, onwendan
owl, úle
own, v., ágan
own, adj., ágen, swǽs
ox, oxa

P

pain, weorc, sárnis, oncýð, angsumnis
painful, angsum
paint (draw), ámǽtan, átífran
pale, blác
pallor, blácung
palm-twig, palmtwig
pan, panne
parents, ildran
park, pearruc
part, dǽl
partly, be sumum dǽle
partner, hlytta
pass (one's life), ádreógan
passage, oferfǽreld
passion, hátheortnis
passionate, hátheort
path, pæð, stíg, gelád
patience, geþyld
patient, geþyldig
patriarch, heáhfæder
pavilion, geteld, træf
pay, gildan
pay for, gebétan
payment, sceatt
peace, grið, freód, frið, sibb
peaceful, sibbsum, gesibbsum
peace-oath, friðáð
pebble, papolstán
peel, screádian
penetrate, þurhþyrelian, þurhwadan
penny, pening, penig
people, þeód, cneóris, folc; leóda, pl.
people, belonging to the, folcisc
pepper, pepor
perceive, ongitan, gefrédan
perfect, fullfremed
perfect, v., fullfremman
perform, fremian, *w. acc.*, fremman, æfnan, ræfnan, gelǽstan, dreógan, begán
perhaps, húru

peril, þearf, fǽr
period, first, stund, ildu
perish, forweorðan, forsíðian, losian
perjured, forsworen, forlogen
perjurer, mánswara
perjury, áðbryce
permission, leáf, geþáfung
persecute, ehtan, oferfolgian
persecution, ehtnis, hete
persecutor, ehtere, hata, cirichata
person, mann
persuade, tyhtan
perverse, wóhlic, þweorh, wiðerweard
perversity, þweorhnis
pestilence, steorfa
philosopher, úðwita
physician, lǽce
piece, stycce
pierce, þyrlian, stingan, þurhdrifan
pierced, þyrel
piercing, þyrelung
piety, æfæstnis
pine, v., pínan
pious, æfæst, godfyrht
pirate, wícing, sǽmann, sǽrinc, brimmann, brimlíðend
pit, pytt, seáð
pitch, pic
pitcher, orc
pith, piða
pity, v., ofhreówan, miltsian, árian
pity, milts, miltsung, ár
place, v., stellan, ásettan, gelogian
place, steall, stede, stow
plain, wang, mearc
plant, s., plant, wyrt
plant, v., plantian
play, plega
play, v., plegian, lácan
pleasant, wynnlic, wynnsum, heóre, getǽse
please, lícian, gelícian, *w. dat.*
pleased with, oflyst, *w. gen.*
pledge, wedd
plight (danger), pliht
plot, v., sirwan
plough, v., erian
pluck, pluccian
plunder, v., berípan, *w. gen.;* rípan, reáfian
plunder, húð, reáfung
plunderer, reáfere
poem, sang
poet, scóp
poetry, leóðsang; *(art of)*, sangcræft

27

point, ord
poison, átor, áttor, unlybba
poisonous, átorbǽre, ǽtren, ǽttren
pomp, prass
poor, earm, unspédig, wanspédig, heán
poor, to be, wǽdlian
poor man, wǽdla, þearfa
pope, pápa
port, port
possess, ágan, geágan, healdan, gewealdan, rómigan (*w. gen.*)
possessions, ǽhta (*pl.*), gestreón
possessor, weard
post, post
pound, pund
pour out, geótan, ágeótan
poverty, wǽdl, irmðu
power, miht, meaht, geweald, onweald, cræft
powerful, ríce, cræftig
praise, herung, lof
praise, v., herian, díran, dýran
pray, gebiddan, *reflex.*
pray for, biddan, *w. acc. of pers. and gen. of thing*
prayer, bén, gebed
preach, bodian, *w. dat.*
preaching, bodung
precious, deóre, dýre
predict, foresecgan
prepare, gearcian, gearwian, girwan, ongirwan
present, adj., andweard
preserve, nerian
press (throng), þringan
press hard, genearwian
pretend, lícettan
prevail, rícsian, ríxian
prevent, forwirnan
price, weorð, wurð
prick, prician
pride, prýte, mód, módignis, hyge, gilp, bælc, gál, gǽlsa, gálscipe, oferhygd, oferméde, ofermetto, ofermód
priest, preóst, sacerd
prince, æðeling, ealdor, brego; *also* fengel, þengel, bealdor, leód, þeóden (*poet.*)
prison, cweartern, clústor
prisoner, rǽpling
proceed, féran
proclaim, ácýðan
produce, forðbringan, tydran
progeny, tuddor, tudor, teám
progress, forðgang

promise, gehát
promise, v., behátan
proof (sign), béhð
property, ágen, ǽht, feoh, feó, ár
prophecy, wítegung
prophesy, wítegian
prophet, wítega, wítga
prophetess, wítegestre
proportion, ondefn, andefn
prosper, spówan, *impers. w. dat.*
prosperity, eád, sǽl
prosperous, eádig
protect, gebeorgan, mundbyrdan, werian, gescildan, friðian, griðian
protection, grið, gescildnis, mund, mundbyrd
protector, helm, mundbora, weriend, gehola
proud, módlic, módig, ofermód, prút, wlanc, heálic
proverb, bigspell
Proverbs, book of, bigspellbóc
provide, tilian, *w. gen. of thing and dat. of person*
provided that, wið ðám ðe
provisions, nest; (*for a journey*), wegnest
prudence, snotornis
prudent, gleáw, gleáwhýdig, ferhðgleáw, snotor
psalm, sealm
psalmist, sealmscóp, sealmwyrhta
psalter, sealtere
public, ǽbere
publicly, openlice
pull, teón, bregdan
punish, wrecan, þráfian
punishment, wíte, wracu, morðor
purchase, s., ceáp
purchase (obtain), gewrixlian
pure, unwemme, clǽne, hlútor, hlúttor, sífre
purify, clǽnsian, gefǽlsian
purity, clǽnnis
purple, adj., pællen
push, scúfan, áscúfan, bescúfan
put on, on dón
put to sleep, áswebban

Q

quake, cwacian
quarrel, v., flítan
quarter (direction), ende
quean, cwén
queen, cwén
quell, cwellan

quench (*fire*), ácwencan
question, v., befrignan
quick, arod, snell; (*living, alive*), cwic
quicken (*vivify*), gelífffæstan
quickly, hraðe, hrædlice, snúde, ardlice, tímlice
quiet, s., stillnis
quoth, cwæð

R

race (*kin*), cynn, mennisc ; (*lineage*), strenge ; (*progeny*), teám
race (as in *mill-race*), ræs
raid, rád
rain, regen
rain, shower of, regenscúr
rain, v., rínan
raise, hebban ; (*raise up*), áhebban
rake, s., raca, race
ram, ramm, romm ; (*batteringram*), ramm
rampart, weall
rank, s., æðelu, gebyrd, hád, geþyngðo, geþyncð
rank, of high, weorð, wirð
rank, adj., ranc
ransom, álísan
rare, seldcúð, sellic
rash, wanhýdig
rather (*sooner*), hraðor ;—*he would rather,* him leófre wæs
ravage, hergian, forhergian, oferhergian, íðan
ravaging, forhergung
raven, hræfn
raw, hreáw
ray of light, leóma, scíma
reach, geræcan
read, rædan, árædan
reading, rædung
ready, gearc, gearo, fús ;—*ready to depart,* síðes fús
reap, rípan
reaper, rípere
rear, áræran
receive, onfón, *w. gen., acc.,* or *instr.;* underfón ; (*food*), þicgan
reck, récan, meornan
reckless, réceleás
reckon, recenian, tellan
reconcile, geséman
record, gemynd
recover (*rescue*), hreddan
recover (*from disease*), gewirpan, gewyrpan

recovery (*from trouble*), wirpe
red, reád
redeem, lísan, álísan
reed, hreód
reek (*vapour*), réc
re-establish, geedstaðelian
reflect, smeágan, smeán ; beþencan, *reflex.*
refuse, forsacan, sceorian
refute, álecgan
region, landscipe
reign, rícsian, ríxian
reindeer, hrán
reject, ácweðan
rejoice, fægnian, gefeohan, geblissian
related, gesibb
relationship, sibb
relative, s., sibbling
relax, intr., tóslúpan
release, lísan, álísan
relinquish, ofgifan, oflætan
remain, restan, lífan, belífan, ætstandan
remains, láf
remedy, bót
remember, gemyngian ; gemunan (*poet.*)
remind, gemyngian
remove, áfirran
rend, hrendan
render, ágifan
renew, geniwian, geedniwian
reparation, bót
repent, hreówsian, behreówsian, dædbétan ;—*repent of* (*be sorry for*), ofþyncan, *impers., w. dat. of pers. and gen. of thing*
repents, it, hreóweð
repentance, hreówsung, dædbót
represent, getácnian
reproach, ætwítan, *w. dat. of pers.*
reproach, s., edwít
reproval, þreágung, þreáung, þreápung, þreátung
reprove, þráfian, þreápian, þreátian, þreágan, þreán
request, bén
requital, wiðerleán
requite, gildan, forgildan, gelcánian
rescue, hreddan, áhreddan
resist, forstandan ; wiðsettan, *w. dat.,* wiðstandan, *w. dat.*
resolute, ánræd
resolution, ánrædnis
resound, hlimman

respite, first
rest, rest
rest, v., restan
restless, unstille, wæfre
restore, eft ágifan
restrain oneself, stíran, *refl.*
resurrection, ǽrist
retainer, mann, maguþegn, híred-
    mann, híremann, geselda, dryht-
    guma
retainers, body of, folgoð, dryht,
    duguð
retreat, wiðertrod
return, eftsíð
return, v., cirran, *reflex.;* gehwirfan,
    intrans.
reveal, onhlídan, geopenian
revelation, onwrigennis
revenge, wracu
reverence, mǽð
revile, leahtrian
reward, méd, leán, edleán, wiðer-
    leán
reward, v., geleánian
rhyme, rím
rib, ribb
rich, ríce, eádig, spédig, welig
riches, wela (*often in pl.* welan);
    spéd, blǽd
rid, hreddan
riddle, rǽdels
ride, rídan
rider, ridda
ridge, hrycg
right (hand or side), swíðre
right, riht, *adj. and sb.*
righteous, rihtwís, rihtlic, rihtwíslic
righteousness, rihtwísnis
rightly, rihte, rihtlice
rim, rima
rime, hrím
rind, rind
ring, hring, beág
ripe, rípe
ripe, to become, gerípian
rise, rísan ;—*rise high*, hlifian ;—
    rise as dust, stincan ;—*rise up*,
    upástígan ;—*(raise oneself)*, áræ̂r-
    an, *reflex.*
rising (of the sun), upgang
risk, genéðan, *w. instrum.*
river, eá, é, streám
river-bank, eástæð
road, weg, strǽt ; *see raid*
roar, rárian
rob, reáfian
robber, reáfere

robbery, reáflác, stalu, strúdung
robe, reáf, hrægl, girla, wǽd, ge-
    wǽde
rock, clúd, stán
rocky, clúdig
rod, gird
roe, rá
roll, wealwian, wealcan ; *intrans.*
    windan
rood, ród
roof, hróf
rook, hróc
room, rúm
roomy, rúm
roost (hen-roost), hróst
root, wyrt, wyrtruma
root up, áwyrtwalian
rope, ráp, sál
rose, róse
rot, rotian
rough, hreóh, hreó, unsméðe
round about, ymbútan
row, s. (order), ráw
row, v., rówan ;—*row round*, be-
    rówan
royal, cynelic ;—*royal family*, cyne-
    cynn
rue, hreówan
ruin, v., ámirran
ruined, forloren
rule, rícsian, ríxian, wealdan, rǽdan
rule (dominion), onweald ;—*(of con-
    duct)*, regol
ruler, rǽdend, wealdend
rules, breach of, regolbryce
rules, according to, regollice
ruminate, eodorcan
run, hleápan, irnan, beirnan, ærn-
    an ;—*run aground (of ships)*,
    ásittan
run away, æthleápan
rune, rún
rush, rǽs
rush, v., rǽsan
rust, rust
ruth, hreówð

S

sack, sacc, sæcc
sacrifice, lác
sacrifice, v., offrian, blótan
sad, sár, sárig, sárlic, geómor, hreów,
    hreó, unrót, dreórig
saddle, sadol
sadness, dreórignis, unrótnis
safe (unbetrayed), unswicen

safety, gebeorg
sagacious, gescádwís
sagaciously, gescádwíslice
sagacity, gescádwísnis
sail, segel
sail, v., seglian
sailor, lidmann, flota, flotmann
saint, hálga, sanct
sake, intinga;—for his sake, for his
    ðingum; and see strife
sallow, salu
salmon, leax
salt, s. and adj., sealt
salute, hálettan
salve (to anoint), sealfian
same, self;—the same, ilca; and see
    similarly
sanctuary, place of, friðstow, hálig-
    nis
sand, sand
sap, sæp
Saturday, sæternesdæg
save, nerian, áhreddan, gebeorgan
saviour, hǽlend, nergend
saw (a saying), sagu, cwide
say, secgan, cweðan, gecweðan
saying, cwide, sagu
scarcely, uneáðe, earfoðlice
scathe, sceððan
scatter abroad, strédan
science, lár
scrape, scafan
scribe, bócere
scripture, gewrit
sea, sǽ, mere, mereflód, flot, holm
sea-bird, brimfugol
seal (animal), seolh, seol
seam, seám
sear (to wither up), forseárian
seat, stól, setl
second, óðer
secret, dirne, dígol
secretly, dígollice
secular, woruldcund
secure (fasten), befæstan
secure, fæst
security, fæstnung, wǽr
sedge, secg
sedition, stric
seduce, forspanan
see, geseón, sceáwian; (perceive),
    ongitan;—see over, oferseón
seed, sǽd
seek, sécan, feccan
seem, þyncan, impers., w. dat.
seethe, seóðan
seize, fón, befón, niman, gelǽcan

seldom, seldon
self, self
sell, sellan, cípan, cýpan, beceápian
send, sendan, ásendan;—send for,
    ofsendan;—send forth, onsendan,
    lǽtan
sense, andgit
separate, syndrig
separate, v., tótwǽman;—separate
    from, getwǽfan, w. gen.
sepulchre, lícrest, moldærn
serf, þrǽl
sermon, lárspell
serpent, wyrm
servant, þegen, þeów, þeówa, cnapa,
    ambihtscealc
servant (female), ðínen, ðeówen
serve, þrówian, þeówan; þegnian,
    w. dat.
service, þeówotdóm, þegenscipe, þeg-
    nung, þénung
servile, cirlisc
serving-man, þegnungmann
servitude, þeówot, þeówdóm
set, settan;—set down, settan;—set
    forth (write), gesettan; (to place),
    ástellan
settle (people), gesettan; (intrans.),
    sittan
seven, seofon
sevenfold, seofonfeald
seventh, seofoða
seventy, hundseofontig
severe, swíð, swíðlic, stíð, stíðlic,
    þearl, hefig, strang
severely, þearle, þearllice, strǽclice,
    unsófte
sew, siwian
shade, scúa
shadow, scadu, sceadu, scúa
shaft, sceaft; (handle), helf
shake, scacan, sceacan, áscacan,
    cweccan, ácweccan; (wag), wag-
    ian
shake off (sleep), tóbredan
shall, I, ic sceal
shame, scamu
shamefully, bismerlice
shank, sceanc, sceanca, scanca
shape, scippan
share, scearu
sharp, scearp, scearplic, heard
sharpness, scearpnis
shave, scafan
she, heó (cf. seó)
sheaf, sceáf
shear, sceran

sheath, sceáð
shed, geótan;—*shed tears*, ágeótan;
(*separate*), sceádan
shedding of blood, gyte
sheep, sceáp
sheep-fold, scépen
sheer; see bright
sheet, sceát
shell, scell
shelter, hleó, sceát
shepherd, hirde
shew, éwan, eówan, æteówan, ge-
    tácnian
shield, scild, bord; (*poet.*), lind,
    rand
shield (*protect*), ymbbeorgan
shilling, scilling
shin-bone, scinbán
shine, scínan, blícan, lixan
ship, scip, ceól, æsc, lid, mereheng-
    est
ships, to provide with, gescipian
shire, scír
shoal (*of fish*), scolu
shoe, scó
shoot, sceótan; — *shoot through*,
    þurhsceótan
shooter, sceótend
shooting, scyte
shore, stæð, ófer, strand
short, sceort
shot (*arrow*), gesceot
shot (*reckoning*), gesceot
should, I, ic sceolde, ic scolde
shoulder, eaxl, sculdor
shove, scúfan, áscúfan
shower, scúr;—(*of rain*), regenscúr
shred, screádian
shrew-mouse, screáwa
shrift, scrift
shrine, scrín
shrink up, forscrincan
shrive, scrífan
shroud, scrúd
shun, onscunian
shut, scyttan
shuttle (*cf.* A.S. scyttel, *a bolt, bar*)
sick, seóc, mettrum
sicken, gesíclian
side, síde, healf;—*on this side of*,
    beheonan, *w. dat.;—on all sides*,
    æghwanon;—*from all sides*, ge-
    hwanon
sieve, sife
sift, siftan
sigh, sícan
sighing, sícetung

sight, gesihð
sign, tácen, beácen
signification, getácnung
signify, getácnian, secgan
silent, to be, swígian; *sometimes w.
    gen.*
silk, seolc
sill, syll
silly (*cf.* A.S. gesælig, *happy*)
silver, seolfor;—*made of*, silfren
similarly, swá same
simple, bilewit
simplicity, bilewitnis
simply, bilewitlice
sin, v., syngian, ágyltan, scyldgian
sin, synn, scyld, gylt
since, siððan, ðæs ðe, nú
sincere, inweard
sinful, synfull, forsyngod
sing, singan, galan, ásingan, ágalan
single, ánlípe
sink, sígan, ásígan ; (*causal*), senc-
    an
sinner, gyltend
sister, sweostor, swustor ; *pl.* ge-
    sweostor
sit, sittan
six, six
sixth, sixta
sixty, sixtig
size, micelnis
skilful, fród
skilfully, listum
skill, cræft, list, searu
skin, fell
sky, swegel ; (*poet.*), rodor
slack, sleac
slander, hól
slaughter, slege, sleaht, wæl, wæl-
    sleaht, wælsliht, fill ;—*slaughter,
    greedy for*, wælgífre
slave, þeów
slay, sleán, ofsleán, fillan
slaying, sliht
sleep, slæp, swefen, swefn
sleep, slæpan, onslæpan, swefan,
    hnæppian ;—*put to sleep*, áswebb-
    an
sleeplessness, slæpleást
slide, slídan (*Somner*)
slight, gehwæde
slightly, hwónlice
slime, slím
sling, liðere
slink, slincan
slip off, áwindan
slippery, slipor

slit, slítan
sloe, slá (Lye)
slope, hlinian
sloth, ásolcennis
slow, slaw, læt, sǽne
slumber, slumerian (Lye)
small, smæl, mǽte, medmicel ·
smear, smerian
smirk, smercian
smite, smítan
smith, smið
smithy, smiððe
smock, smocc
smoke, v., smeócan
smoke, þrosm, réc
smooth, sméðe
snail, snægl
snake, snaca, nædre
snatch, gegrípan
sneak (to creep), snícan
snow, snáw
so, swá ;—so much, tó ðæm, tó ðæs
soap, sápe
sock, socc
sodden, soden ; see seethe
soft, sófte, hnesc
soften, gelíðian, gehnescian, onwǽc-
  an
softly, sófte, hnesclice
softness, hnescnis
some, sum, náthwilc;—some one, sum
something, hwæthwegu
sometimes, hwílum, þragum
somewhat, hwæt, hwón, hwéne
son, sunu, mǽg, maga, magu
song, sang, gidd, leóð
soon, sóna, hrædlic, lungre ;—as
  soon as, sóna swá
sooth (true, truth), sóð
sooth, in, tó sóðe
sore, sár, adj. and sb.
sorely, sáre
sorrow, sorg, sár
sorrow, v., sorgian
sorrowful, sorgfull
sorry, sárig
soul, sáwul
sound, s., són, hleóðor, sweg,
  bearhtm
sound (healthy), gesund, onsund
sound (unhurt), gesund, gesundfull
sound of the sea, sund
soundness (health), onsundnis
sour, súr
south, from the, súðan
south of, wið súðan, w. acc.
southern, súðerne

south part, súðdǽl
southward, adj., súðeweard
southwards, súð
sovereignty, ealdordóm
sow, sáwan, sprengan
sower, sáwere
space, rýmet ; (of time), fæc, first
spacious, rúm, ginn
spare, sparian
spark, spearca
sparrow, spearwa
speak, sprecan, specan, cweðan,
  mǽlan, maðelian, hleóðrian
spear, spere, gár, franca, daroð,
  wælsteng ; (poet.), æsc ;—spear-
  point, ord
spear-shaft, æscholt
special, synderlic
specially, synderlice
speech, sprǽc, mǽl, cwide, cwide-
  gidd
speechless, cwideleás
speed (success), spéd
spell; see narrative
spend, forspendan
spew, spíwan
spill; see destroy
spin, spinnan
spindle, spindel
spirit, gást
spiritual, gástlic
spit, spittan, spyttan
splendid, wrǽttlic
splendidly, wrǽttlice
sponsor, godsibb
sport, v., lácan
spread abroad, intrans., áspringan
spring (Lent), lencten
spring, springan
spring forth, onspringan
spring up, áspringan
sprinkle, sprengan
sprinkle over, geondsprengan
spurn, spurnan (Somner), spornettan
square, feówerscíte
stab, þýdan ;—stab to death, ofsting-
  an
staff, stæf
stain, wamm
stained, fág, fáh
stake, staca, stocc, steng
stall (for cattle), steall, scépen
stand, standan ; (up), ástandan ;
  (still), óðstandan
star, steorra, tungol
starboard, steórbord
stare, starian

stark (*severe, rough*), stearc
starve; see die
state (*condition*), hád
stature, wæstm
stay (*remain*), wunian
stead, stæl, stede
steadfast, stedefæst
steal, stelan
steal along (*move noiselessly*), be-
   stelan
steam, steám
steed, stéda
steel, stíl
steep, steáp
steeple, stépel, stýpel
steer, stíran
stem (*trunk*), stemn
stench, stenc
step, steppan
sterility, unwæstm
stern, *adj.*, stirne, stirnmód
stick, stocc
stiff, stíð
stile, stígel
still, *adj.*, stille; *adv.*, git, nú git,
   ðá git, forð
stillness, stillnis
sting, stingan
stink, stincan, reócan
stir, styrian, hréran
stirrup, stígráp
stock (*stick*), stocc
stone, stán
stone, made of, stǽnen
stone to death, oftorfian
stone-wall, stánweall
stony, stǽniht
stool; see seat
storm, storm, unweder, hríð
storm, *v.*, styrman
story, spell, stǽr
stout-hearted, swíðmód
straight on, on gerihte
strand, strand
strand (*a ship*), beebbian
strange, fremde, elfremede, ælfrem-
   ede, sellic; (*unrelated to*), un-
   gesibb
straw, streáw
stream, streám
street, strǽt
strength, strengu, mægen, þryðu,
   þrymm, eafoð
strengthen, trymian, trymman
strengthening, trymmung
stretch, streccan, þenian; ástreccan
   (*reflex.*)

strew, streáwian
strife, stríð, gewinn, sacu
strike, sleán; (*off*), of ásleán ; (*down*),
   gesleán
strip of, bestrípan, *w. gen.*
stroke, sweng, dynt
stroke, *v.*, strácian
strong, strang, stranglic, strenglic,
   stíð, trum, swíð, dyhtig, þyhtig,
   þryðlic; (*poet.*), eácen
subject, *v.*, underþeódan
subjection, underþeódnis
succeed (*prosper*), spówan, *impers.*
   w. dat.
success, forðgang, spéd
successor, æftergenga
such, swilc, ðilc
such a one, swilc
such...as, swilc...hwilc
suck, súcan
suckle, gesýcan
suddenly, fǽringa, fǽrlice
suffer (*endure*), þolian; (*feel pain*),
   þrowian, cwilmian; (*allow*), ge-
   þáfian
suffering, þrowung
suffice, genyhtsumian
suffices, *it*, geneah
sufficiency, genyhtsumnis
sufficient, genyhtsum
suit, *v.*, gedafenian
suitable, gerisenlic, gelimplic, déflic
sully, besylian
sulphur, swefl
sulphurous, sweflen
summer, sumor
summon, bannan, gelangian, gelað-
   ian, ofsendan, stefnian
sun, sunne
sunbeam, sunnbeám
Sunday, sunnandæg
sunder; see apart
sundry, syndrig
sup, súpan
supply (*stock*), onsteall ; (*material*),
   feorm
support, áberan
surface, brerd ; (*of the earth*), sceát
surge, brimwilm, ýð
surround, begán, behringan, be-
   windan ; (*ride round*), berídan ;
   —(*a town*), útan besittan
survey, sceáwian
surveying, sceáwung
sustenance, bigwist, bigleofa, fóstor
swain, swán
swallow (*bird*), swealwe, swalewe

swallow, swelgan, *w. instrum.*
swan, swan
swarm, swearm
swarthy, sweart
swear, áswerian
sweat, swát
sweep away, forswápan
sweet, swéte
sweetness, swétnis
swell, swellan
swell greatly, tóswellan
swift, swift
swim, swimman
swimming, sund
swine, swín
swinge (beat), swingan
swoon, swima
sword, sweord, swurd, seax, méce, heoru, heoruwǽpen, bill, hildebill, wígbill ; (*poet.*), brand, beaduleóma
sword-stroke, sweordgeswing

T

table, beód, bord
tail, steort, tægl
take, niman, fón, gefeccan ;—*away*, ániman ; ætbregdan, *w. dat. ;—* (*a city*), ábrecan ; (*as food*), þicgan
tale (story), getæl
tame, tam
taper (candle), tapor
tar, teru
tart (acrid), teart
teach, tǽcan, lǽran
teacher, láreów
team; see progeny
tear, s., teár
tear, v. teran, slítan ;—*asunder*, tóteran
tease, tǽsan
teem, tíman
tell, secgan, ásecgan, gecýðan ; *see reckon*
temperance, forhæfednis
tempest, gewider
temple, tempel
tempt, fandian
temptation, costung
tempting, fandung
ten, tín, týn
tender, týdre
tent, geteld, teld, búrgeteld, træf
tenth, teóða
term of military service, stefn, stemn

terrible, gryrelic, atol
territory, éðel
terror, gryre, bróga, óga
test, cunnian, gecunnian, áfandian
testimony, gewitnis
than, ðonne, *w. comparatives*
thane, þegen
thank, v., þancian
thanks, þanc ; (*thanks to God*), Godes þances
that, ðæt, ðætte, ðe ;—*in order that*, for ðám ðæt
thatch, s., þæc
thaw, þáwan
the, se (*m.*), seó (*f.*), ðæt (*n.*)
the...the (with comparatives), swá... swá
the greater, ðý mára (*correlatively*)
thee, ðé, ðec
theft, þífð
their, hira
them, hí, hig (*acc.*); him (*dat.*)
then, ðonne, ðá, ðǽr
thence, ðanon ; (*from that cause*), ðæs
there, ðǽr
therefore, ðý, for ðý, for ðám
these, ðás
they, hí, hig
*they were...*ðæt wǽron...
thick, þicce
thief, þeóf, sceaða
thigh, þeóh
thin, þynne
thine, ðín
thing, þing, wiht, wuht
think, þencan, hycgan, gemyntan ; —*of*, þencan ;—*about*, hogian
third, þridda
thirst, v., þyrstan
thirst, þurst
thirty, þritig, þrittig
thirtyfold, þritigfeald
this, ðes
thistle, þistel
thither, ðider, ðiderweardes, ðiderweard, ðǽr
thong, þwang
thorn, þorn
those, ðá
thou, ðú
though, ðeáh, ðéh ; *though...yet*, ðeáh ðe...ðeáh
thought, geþóht, þanc, geþanc, módgeþóht, módgeþanc, inngeþanc, gehygd
thoughtful, þancol, þancolmód

thousand, þúsend
thousands, in, þúsendmælum
thrall, þræl
thrash, þerscan
thread, þræd
threat, beót
threaten, þreágan, þreán, þreátian
threatening, þreágung, þreáung
three, þreó, þrí, þrý
thresh, þerscan
thrice, þriwa
thrill; see pierce
throat, þrotu
throne, stól, setl, cynesetl, þrymm-
  setl
throng, geþrang, menigu
throng, v., þringan
through, þurh
throughout, þurh, geond
throw, weorpan, wurpan, beweorp-
  an;—*away,* áweorpan [þráwan =
  to twist]
thumb, þúma
thunder, þunor
Thursday, þunresdæg
thus, ðus
tide; see time
tile, tigele
till, v., tilian
timber; see building
time, tíd, tíma, hwíl, mæl, stund,
  þrag; (*occasion*), sæl, cirr;—
  time (space of), fæc;—*from time
  to time,* stundum;—(*how many
  times*), síð;—*at no time,* náhwær
time, wrong (unsuitable season),
  untíma
tin, tinn
tinder, tynder
tired, méðe, wérig
to, tó
toad, táde
to-day, tó dæg
toe, tá
together, tógædere, ætgædere, on
  geador, ætsomne, endemes, sam-
  od
toil, earfoð, geswinc
toil, winnan
token, tácen, tácn.
toll, toll
tomb, byrgen
tongs, tange (*pl.* tangan.)
tongue, tunge
too, tó
tool, tól
tooth, tóð

top, topp, copp
touch, hrepian, hrínan
tough, tóh
torment, wíte, susl, tintreg
torment, v., wítnian, tintregian
towards, tóweard, ongeán, ongén;
  tógeánes, w. dat.; wið, w. dat.,
  acc., or gen.;—*towards heaven,*
  wið ðæs heofones weard
tower, stípel
town, tún
track, spor, gang, lást, swæð, swaðu
track, to make a, spyrian
traitor, wærloga
transform, forscippan
transitory, hwílwende, hwílwendlic,
  læne
translate, wendan, áwendan, árecc-
  an
translater, wealhstód
trappings, gerædc, hyrst
travel, faran, áfaran
traverse, geondfaran, geondhweorf-
  an, geondlácan, oferfaran, ofer-
  gán, þurhfaran, þurhirnan, tredan,
  metan
treacherous, lytig, swicol, fácenfull
treacherous, to be, swician
treachery, ungetreówð, fácen, searu,
  searucræft
tread, tredan
treason, hláfordswice
treasure, goldhord, hord, hordfæt,
  sinc, máðum, mádm
treaty, wær
tree, treów, beám
tremble, bifian
trespass, forwyrcan, *reflex.,* ágyltan
trial, fandung
tribe, mægð, cneóris
tribute, gafol, sceatt, nídgild
trick, wrenc
trim (strengthen), trymman
trinity, þrínis
troop, féða, flocc, gemang, heáp,
  hlóð, gefylce, getrum, getruma,
  sweót, þreát, werod, worn;—*by
  troops,* floccmælum
trouble, s., gedréfednis, bysgu, ge-
  winn, weá
troubled, gedréfed
trough, trog, troh
true, sóð, sóðfæst, treówe, riht;
  (*faithful*), trywe
truly, sóðlice
trust (in), treówian, truwian, w. dat.
trusty, gecost

truth, sóð, sóðfæstnis, treówð
try, fandian, áfandian
tub, cyfu
Tuesday, Tiwes dæg
tumult, gebland, gewinn
tun, tunne
tunic, tunece
turbid, *to become*, drusian
turf, turf
turn, wendan, áwendan, cirran, gehwirfan, gehweorfan; (*become*), wendan; *intrans.*, windan
turn, *in*, wrixendlice
tusk, tusc, tóð
twain, twegen (*masc.*)
twelfth, twelfta
twelve, twelf
twenty, twentig
twice, tuwa
twig, twig
twin, getwisa;—*twins*, getwinne
twine, twín
twinkle, twinclian
twist, windan, þráwan
twit, ætwítan, edwítan
two, twegen, *masc.*, twá, *fem. and neut.*
type, getácnung

U

udder, úder
unallowed, unálífed
unanimous, ánmód
unanimously, ánmódlice
unawares, on ungearwe
unbaptized, ungefullod
unbelief, ungeleáffulnis
unbelieving, ungeleáffull, geleáfleás
unburnt, unforbærned
uncle, eám
unconsciously, ungewisses
uncouth; see unknown
uncover, onwreón, onwríðan; (*unwind*), unwindan
undefended, firdleás
undefiled, ungewemmed, unwemme
under, under, *w. dat. and acc.*
understand, ongitan, oncnáwan, forstandan, understandan
understanding, gewitt
unhappiness, ungesælð
unhappy, ungesælig
unhealthy, wanhál
unite (*draw together*), geánlǽcan
unity, ánnis
unknown, uncúð

unlawful, unálífed
unless, nemne, nefne, búton
unlike, ungelíc
unlock, onlúcan
unmindful, ungemyndig
unopposed, unbefohten
unreasoning, ungewittig
unrighteousness, unrihtwísnis
unsold, unbebóht
unstable, tealt
unsuitable, ungerisenlic
unsuitably, ungerisenlice
until, óð, *usu. w. acc.*
until, *conj.*, óð ðæt, óð
unworthily, unweorðlice
up, up; *adv.*, uppe
upon, onufan, *w. dat.*, onuppan, *w. dat.;* uppon, *w. dat. and acc.*
upwards, up
us, ús
use, notu, nytt
use, *v.*, brúcan, *w. gen.;* neótan, *w.gen.;—use up* (*consume*),genotian
used to, *to be*, willan
useful, nyttwirðe
useless, unnytt, ídel
usual, gewunelic
utility, nytt
uttermost, ýtemest

V

vaguely, unfæstlice
vain, ídel;—*in vain*, on ídelnisse
vale (*open broad valley*), slæd
valley, denu, dæl
valour, dryhtscipe
vane, fana
vapour, steám, þrosm
variegated, fáh, fág
various, mislic, mistlic, missenlic, syndrig
vat, fæt
venerable, árweorð
venture on, genéðan
verily, sóðlice
verse, fers
vertebra, bánhring
very, swíðe, for, full, þearle;—*very old*, oreald
vessel, fæt, fætels, cyfu, cylle
vice, uncyst, unsidu, unþeáw
victorious, sigefæst, sigoreádig
victory, sige, sigor, hréð
vigorously, stranglice
vilify, hirwan, bismerian

village, tún, castel
vineyard, wíngeard .
violate, tóbrecan
violence, níd
violent, hetelic, hetol, hǽst
violently, hetelice
virgin, mægden, mǽden, mægð, fǽmne ; (*poet.*), meówle
virginity, mægðhád
virtue, cyst, mægen, árfæstnis
virtuous, cystig, árfæst
visible, gesíne
visit, sécan ; neósan, *w. gen.*
visitation, neósung
vital, líflic
vixen, fyxen
voice, stefn, stemn, gereord
voluntarily, selfwilles

W

wade, wadan
wag, wagian
waggon, wægn
wailing, þoterung
wain; see waggon
wait, andbídian ;—*for*, onbídan ; bídan, *w. gen.;—upon*, folgian
wake, wacan
walk, wealcan
wall, weall, wah
wallow, wealwian
wall-stone, weallstán
walrus, horshwæl
wan, wann
wander, scríðan, wandrian
wandering, *adj.*, wæfre
wane, wanian
wanton, gálmód, gálferhð
wantonness, gǽlsa
war, wíg, winn, gewinn, gúð, hild, heaðu, sacu, orlege, unfrið : (*poet.*), beadu
ward, weard
war-expedition, heresíð
war-horn, gúðhorn
warily, wærlice
warm, wearm
warn, gewearnian
warning, wearnung
warning, to take, warnian, *reflex.*
warrior, guma, cempa, wíga, wígend, oretta, dreng, freca, hyse, gárberend, sceótend, gúðfreca, gúðrinc, heáðurinc ; herewǽða, hildedeór, hilderinc, wǽpenwíga, beadurinc, firdrinc, lindhæbben-

de, lindwígend, randwíga, randwígend, folcwíga, hagustealdmonn, sweordfreca, wǽlwulf ; (*poet.*), byrnwíga, byrnwígend, rinc, hæle, hæleð, beorn, eorl, þegen, secg
war-song, hildeleóð, gúðleóð
wary, wær
was, wæs
wash, þweahan, þweán, áþweán, wacsan
wasp, wæps, wesp
waste, wéste
waste, to lay, wéstan, áwéstan
watch, *s.*, weard
watch, wæccan ; *intrans.*, wacian ;—*over*, eahtian
watchful, wæccende
water, wæter, lagu
wave, wǽg, waðum, ýð
wax, *s.*, weax
wax (*to grow*), weaxan
way, weg
way, to clear a, gerýman
wayfaring, wegfarende
we, wé
weak, wác, untrum, wanhál, unmihtig
weak, to become, wácian
weaken, gelísan
weakness, uncræft, untrumnis ;— *weakness of mind*, wácmódnis
weal; see wealth
wealth, wela (*often in pl.* welan).
wealthy, welig
wean, wenian
weapon, wǽpen
wear, werian
weary, wérig, méðe
weasel, wesle
weather, weder
weave, wefan
web, webb
wed; see pledge
wedge, wecg
Wednesday, Wódnesdæg
weed, weód
weeds (*garments*), wǽda, *pl.*
week, wicu, wucu
ween, wénan
weep, wépan, reótan, greótan, grǽtan
weeping, wóp
weevil, wifel
weigh, wǽgan
weird; see fate
welkin (*sky*), wolcen

well, s., willa
well, wel, tela
Welsh, Welsc
wen, wenn
wend; see turn
went, eode
were, wǽron
west, west
west, from the, westan
west of, be westan, *w. dat.*
west quarter, westdǽl
westwards, westlang, westweard, west
west wind, westanwind
wet, wǽt
wet, v., wǽtan
wether, weðer
whale, hwæl
whale-fisher, hwælhunta
whale-fishery, hwælhuntað
what, hwæt, hwilc
wheat, hwǽte
wheel, hwcól
wheeze, hwǽsan
whelk, weolc
whelp, hwelp
when, hwanne, hwænne, ðǽr, tó ðæs ðe ; (*when that*), ðá ðá, mid ðám ðe, mid ðý
when...then, ðonne...ðonne, ðá...ðá
whence, hwanon
where, hwǽr, hwar, ðǽr
wherefore, for hwý
wherever, swá hwider swá
whet, hwettan
whether, hwæðer
whether...or, sam...sam
whey, hwǽg
which, hwilc
which of the two, hwæðer
whichever, swá hwæðer swá
while, ðenden
while, s., hwíl
whilst, ðá hwíle ðe
whine, hwínan
whirlpool, wǽl
whisper, hwisprian
whistle, hwistlian
whit, wiht
white, hwít, blác
whither, hwider, hwǽr, ðǽr
whithersoever, swá hwider swá
who, ðe, se ðe, se ; hwá?
whoever, swá hwilc swá
whole, hál, onsund
whoop, hwópan
whose, hwás

why, hwý, hwæt
wicked, lyðre, mánfull, fracod, inwidd, árleás
wickedly, árleáslice, mánfullice
wickedness, yfel, yfelnis, mán
wide, wíd, síd, ginn
widely, wíde, síde
widely known, wídcúð
widen, gerýman
widow, widuwe, wuduwe
wield (a weapon), wealdan
wife, gebedde, wíf
wight, wiht
wild, wilde
wilderness, wésten
wile, wíle
will, s., willa, gewill ;—*of one's own will,* selfwilles;—*against his will,* his unþances
willingly, georne, geornlice, lustlice
willingness, willsumnis
willow, wilig
win, gewinnan ; (*by fighting*), gefeohtan
wind, s., wind
wind, windan
windy, windig
wine, wín
wing, feðer
wink, wincian
winnow, windwian
winsome (pleasant), wynnsum
winter, winter
wire, wír
wisdom, wísdóm, snotornis
wise, wís, witig, snotor, fród, rǽdfæst, hygeþancol
wise, s. (way), wíse
wise man, wita, wítega, wítga
wish, willa
wish, v., willan, wýscan ;—*for,* hogian, *w. gen.*, gelystan, *impers. w. acc. of pers. and gen. of thing*
wish, not to, nyllan
wit, s., gewitt
wit (to know), witan
witch, wicce
with, mid
wither, forweornian, forseóðan
withhold, forhealdan ; gestíran, *w. dat. of pers. and gen. of thing;* ofteón,*w. instrum.;* wirnan,wyrnan, *w. gen. (and also w. dat. of person)*
within, oninnan, *w. dat.*, wiðinnan, *w. dat.; adv. (also as prep. w. dat.)*, innan, binnan

39

without, wiðútan, *w. dat.;* búton,
w. dat.
witness, gewitnis, gewita
woad, wád
woe, wá *(exclamation)*
woe, weá
woe, sign of, weátácen
woe, tidings of, weáspell
wolf, wulf
woman, wíf, wífmann ; (*poet.*), ides
womb, innoð; (*belly*), wamb
wonder, wundor
wonder at, v., wundrian, *w. gen.*
wonderful, wundorlic
wont, to be, gewunian
wonted, gewunelic
woo, wógian
wood, treów ; (*forest*), wudu, holt,
holtwudu, weald
wool, wull
word, word
work, weorc
work, v., wyrcan
worker, wyrhta
world, middangeard, woruld ;—*cir-
cuit of the*, ymbhwirft
worldly, woruldlic
worm, wyrm, maða
worse, to become, wirsian
worse, wirsa
worship, s., weorðung, wurðung
worship, weorðian, wurðian
worst, wirst
wort, wyrt
worth, s., weorð, wurð ; duguð
worth, to be, dugan
worthy, weorð, wirð
wot, I, ic wát
would, I, ic wolde
wound, wund, dolg ; (*poet.*), benn
wound, forwundian, gesárgian
wounded, dolgwund, wund
woven, gebroden
wreak, wrecan
wreath, wræð
wren, wrænna
wrench, wrencan
wrest, wræstan
wretch, poor, earming

wretched, earm, earmlic, wræcfull
wretchedly, earmlice
wright (worker), wyrhta
wring, wringan
wrist, wrist
write, wrítan
writer, wrítere
writhe, wríðan
writing, gewrit
wrong, unriht, wrang, unrihtlic,
wrangwís
wrong, s., unriht
wroth, wráð
wrought (did work), worhte

Y

yard (court), geard
yard (measure), gerd
yarn, gearn
ye, ge
yea, geá
year, geár, gér ; (*in reckoning time*),
winter
yearn, gernan
yeast, gist
yell, gylian
yellow, geolo
yelp, gelpan
yes, gese, gise
yesternight, gistran niht
yet, ðeáh, ðéh, ðeáhhwæðcre, gén ;
(*w. neg.*), git
yew, íw
yield, sellan ;—*up*, linnan, *w. in-
strum.* [gildan = *to pay*]
yoke, geoc
yolk, geolca
yore, of, geára
yore, days of, firndagas, geárdagas;—
former years, firngeár
you, eów
young, geóng, unweaxen
your, eówer
youth, geóguð ; (*young man*), hyse

Z

zeal, anda, ellen, ellenwódnis

CAMBRIDGE: PRINTED BY C. J. CLAY, M.A. AT THE UNIVERSITY PRESS.

www.ingramcontent.com/pod-product-compliance
Lightning Source LLC
Chambersburg PA
CBHW021446090426
42739CB00009B/1664